Constellations

Social Fictions Series

The titles published in this series are listed at *brill.com/soci*

Constellations

By

Patricia Leavy

BRILL

SENSE

LEIDEN | BOSTON

All chapters in this book have undergone peer review.

Library of Congress Cataloging-in-Publication Data

Names: Leavy, Patricia, 1975- author.
Title: Constellations / by Patricia Leavy.
Description: Leiden ; Boston : Brill Sense, [2021] | Series: Social
  fictions series, 25428799 ; vol. 41
Identifiers: LCCN 2021007388 (print) | LCCN 2021007389 (ebook) | ISBN
  9789004461963 (paperback) | ISBN 9789004461970 (hardback) | ISBN
  9789004461987 (ebook)
Classification: LCC PS3612.E2198 C66 2021 (print) | LCC PS3612.E2198
  (ebook) | DDC 813/.6--dc23
LC record available at https://lccn.loc.gov/2021007388
LC ebook record available at https://lccn.loc.gov/2021007389

ISSN 2542-8799
ISBN 978-90-04-46196-3 (paperback)
ISBN 978-90-04-46197-0 (hardback)
ISBN 978-90-04-46198-7 (e-book)

This book is printed on acid-free paper and produced in a sustainable manner.

ADVANCE PRAISE FOR
CONSTELLATIONS

"Family, love, and trauma are vital aspects of our relational lives. Yet, what (and who) makes up a "family," and what is the "right" way to love? Also, what happens to the family and love we have come to expect and need when trauma invades our lives? Patricia Leavy's *Constellations* immerses readers in the process of exploring these issues. Her latest novel is an accessible story and immerses readers in situations that will lead us to re-examine both how we have lived and the people we have loved. Like the stars that appear in our nighttime skies, people and relationships are forever interconnected. The dynamic love story of Tess and Jack continues!"
– Keith Berry, Ph.D., University of South Florida

"In this gorgeous novel, talented writer Patricia Leavy brings back her unforgettable characters in the third Tess Lee and Jack Miller installation. Tess Lee's motto is to move through darkness into light. In *Constellations*, Tess brings light to family trauma, grief, and missed opportunities. This novel explores the idea of what family—in every sense of the word—can be. The vivid prose and beautifully rendered characters left me filled with hope and a sense of possibility. I highly recommend this book. I read it in one sitting, unable to put it down until I reached the last word."
– Jessica Smartt Gullion, Ph.D., Texas Woman's University

"Tess and Jack are back, and I want to be adopted into this family. *Constellations* is told as a family saga through the arc of the holiday season. There's anger and reconciliation, false fronts abandoned and real connection reestablished, a brush with death and new lives begun. And all the while, people who are thrown together by birth and by happenstance find they can come together to form a constellation of love in all its forms: between partners, among friends, within families. You will want to immerse yourself in the constellation of love and

self-knowledge to imagine the celebrations of Christmas and Easter and of everyday life."
– Eve Spangler, Ph.D., Boston College

"With her incisive sociological eye, Leavy offers another riveting book about the nuances and beauty of mundane interaction, the significance of friendship and family, the ways steadfast love and commitment can withstand adversity, and the growth that can stem from grief, loss, conflict, and success."
– Tony E. Adams, Bradley University

"As an instructor of the practice of social work on both the graduate and undergraduate level, it brings me great joy when I read academic pieces that are tailored to both the learning process and the internalizing of empathy. While reading *Constellations*, I immediately began pondering how I could use this work of art in my Individuals and Families courses, in my Diversity courses, in my Human Behavior and the Social Environment courses, and on and on. Dr. Leavy touches on so many sociological subjects in one beautifully laid out story and hints at the complexities of so many lives that as one turns the last page of the book, you know the healing process has really just begun. So tonight, as you look into the sky and notice that one bright and shiny star, know that there is an entire constellation behind it, and so it is with our clients and our students."
– Renita M. Davis, LICSW, PIP, Troy University

"*Constellations* returns us to the enchanting universe of the world's most successful author, Tess Lee, and former FBI agent Jack Miller. Set during the ever-fraught family season, we begin to see the real challenges inherent in two broken people coming together, where unaddressed past traumas leak into our present to infect our now. Leavy is able to eviscerate you by weaving the deep traumas that Tess and Jack have experienced, traumas that in less-skilled hands would feel like a plot point to drive a narrative forward and then be forgotten by the protagonists once they fall in love. *Constellations* expertly explores the ways in which trauma embeds itself, even

after the happily ever after. Yet, Leavy reminds us that love, in all its forms, is ultimately rewarded by delving more deeply into the ways that Tess's spirit brings an array of wonderful people into her life to become her living comfort blanket, or indeed her constellation, that can only survive through honest communication. There are so many components that demonstrate Leavy's expertise in explicitly and implicitly drawing out the truths at the heart of humanity in today's world in ways we can all relate to, while creating a story that feels incredibly intimate. The reason I keep returning to her work is her talent for writing stories for multiple audiences at multiple levels with a story engaging enough to be an easy read, no matter the intent behind picking it up. In this way, this might be the first novel I have read that is filled with a truly diverse range of images of masculinity, so much so that it becomes essential supplementary reading in any class, especially those focused on gender, masculinity, or trauma, as well as broad fields like sociology, social work, and communication. But at its heart, Leavy's third part of Tess and Jack's story is a novel that must be read because it's too good not to."
– U. Melissa Anyiwo, Ph.D., Curry College, editor of *Gender Warriors: Reading Contemporary Urban Fantasy*

"In the third Tess Lee novel, we see how love is a selfless and self-full act that burns the brightest when we follow our inner light and project that outward. Like the constellations, Tess and Jack show us how love may seem like a random group of stars until it transforms us into the crucial link in a connected pattern of love-filled relationships."
– Sandra L. Faulkner, Ph.D., author of *Poetic Inquiry: Craft, Method and Practice*

"Understanding our feelings can often feel like an extended process of stargazing. With *Constellations*, Patricia Leavy explores this metaphor in family relationships. This follow-up to *Shooting Stars* and *Twinkle* takes a subtler approach than either of its predecessors, turning away from high drama to long strings of quietly electric moments that shimmer like holiday lights. Yet, lest we think this novel is the neatly wrapped stuff of made-for-TV movies, it uses the winter holidays to illuminate

the thick ice trapping the emotions of trauma survivors. Leavy gives the deepest chills in showing readers how even the most healed of heroes can easily fall prey to toxic patterns, and makes us vibrate with familiar frustration at experiences we likely share. Even with their vast resources and genuine love, Tess Lee and Jack Miller cannot escape the essential truism that survivors with feminine qualities often do the work of "finishing" those with masculine ones—until they choose to do it themselves. The lesson here rings all the more clearly for its understated grace: When we consciously make those healing choices to examine and name the complex clusters of simmering energy within us, we come closer to the stars and one another."
– Alexandra "Xan" Nowakowski, Ph.D., MPH, Florida State University

"Especially as someone who has depended upon and often written about the establishment of chosen families, I was even more delighted than usual to reconnect with Tess as she navigates these and other familial themes in *Constellations*. In fact, my delight expanded with each page of this gripping, emotional, at times humorous, and loving story about the complexity that we call love and the possibilities for building love and connection with the self and others over time. *Constellations* is truly a wonderful complement to *Shooting Stars* and *Twinkle*, as well as a beautiful introspective love story in its own right!"
– J. E. Sumerau, Ph.D., The University of Tampa

"*Constellations* is a book about connections, relationships, and the logic of finding patterns in the seemingly random. In this latest work by masterful writer Patricia Leavy, we again reacquaint ourselves with the cast of characters in these stellar stories. Once more, I eagerly sat down to join Tess, Jack, and their coterie of fine friends and loved ones. I eagerly read Leavy's tale of love and family that teaches us the importance of leaning into the love of those who care for you the most. Tess's sparkling literary career is topped only by her grace and deep emotional wisdom, her kindness and spectacular global reach. Tess's stories are alive with light, emerging from the darkness of human experience; they tell of pain and bitter experience redeemed, humanity

and grace. An important lesson from Tess's writing (and by extension, Leavy's) is that the way we treat others is who we become, a lesson never more important than in these trying, turbulent, frightening, and divisive times. In the primary relationship of this series, that of Tess and her husband Jack, we learn the transformational power of love, of unconditional love. This is a relationship we all aspire to have: one of unconditional and steady devotion. Both Tess and Jack have experienced and survived deep, indescribable pain and loss in their lives. They have both had a life of seeking without realizing, existing without living—despite the important and satisfying work they both do very successfully. Their love, as a consequence, is deep and unrelenting, and Leavy's portrayal is sensitive and authentic; their relationship is beautifully drawn. Symbolism and metaphor are powerfully employed in this book, the notion of a constellation reflected in the strong web of ties between dear friends, cherished family, and our beloveds. The pain Leavy writes about is, as she says herself, "laced with infinite hope." The epilogue of this beautiful book brought me to tears, so poignant in its portrayal of an authentic marriage of mutual support, of its flaws and successes, of the trust in the one you love the most who can truly see you. The abject safety of that. The themes, metaphors, and lessons in this book are strongly present and beautifully drawn. The most significant in my reading is about leaning into the love of the people who love you most, whether they be your blood family or the family you have chosen. This theme resonates strongly, again and again throughout this book series, through the relatable experiences and encounters of the characters. Once more, Patricia Leavy has woven her special magic as an accomplished scholar of arts-based research, and written a highly readable, beautifully accessible, wonderfully compelling work of fiction."
– **Alexandra Lasczik, Ph.D., Southern Cross University**

Selected Fiction from Patricia Leavy

Twinkle

Shooting Stars

Candy Floss Collection

Film

Low-Fat Love Stories
By Patricia Leavy and Victoria Scotti

Blue

American Circumstance: Anniversary Edition

Low-Fat Love: Expanded Anniversary Edition

For more information, visit the author's website
www.patricialeavy.com

For all those who left us too soon.
We see you in the stars,
we see you everywhere.

CONTENTS

ACKNOWLEDGEMENTS

Thank you to everyone at Brill | Sense for supporting this book and my growth as an author. Special thanks to John Bennett, Jolanda Karada, Els van Egmond, Henriët Graafland, Caroline van Erp, Evelien van der Veer, and Robert van Gameren. Thank you to the editorial advisory board members of the *Social Fictions* series for your generosity, and to the early reviewers for your kind endorsements. Heartfelt thanks to Shalen Lowell, the world's best assistant, spiritual bodyguard, and friend. Sincere appreciation to Celine Boyle, the world's best writing buddy, for the invaluable feedback. Thank you to Clear Voice Editing for the always phenomenal copyediting services. To my social media community and colleagues, thank you boundlessly for your support. My deep gratitude to my friends, especially Tony Adams, Vanessa Alssid, Melissa Aniywo, Keith Berry, Renita Davis, Pamela DeSantis, Sandra Faulkner, Ally Field, Robert Charles Gompers, Alexandra Lasczik, Laurel Richardson, Xan Nowakowski, Mr. Barry Mark Shuman, Jessica Smartt Gullion, Eve Spangler, and J. E. Sumerau. My love to my parents. Madeline Leavy-Rosen, you are my light and my heart. Mark Robins, you're the best spouse in the world. Thank you for all that words cannot capture. This novel is in loving memory of all those who left us too soon. We see you in the stars, we see you everywhere.

CHAPTER 1

Tess clung to Jack as they sped along the cliffside road on their Harley, winding around the last curve as they approached their house. When they arrived home, Jack carefully took off Tess's helmet, kissed her, and grabbed the bag of fruit they'd bought at the farmers market. She pulled the scrunchie out of her hair, releasing dirty blonde locks down to her waist. They headed inside. "You thirsty, baby?" he asked.

She nodded.

He quickly tapped a coconut, stuck a paper straw in, and handed it to her.

"You've gotten so good at that," she said, taking a sip.

"Yeah, just in time to go back to DC. I can't believe we have to leave our Hawaiian paradise tomorrow morning. We're crazy to leave Maui this time of year."

"I know, baby. But we'll be back in less than three months to throw Omar and Clay the tropical Valentine's Day wedding of their dreams. Besides, it'll be fun to see our friends."

He smiled and kissed her forehead.

"Here, have some," she said, handing him the coconut. "Let's leave the pineapple out. We can grill it tonight for our Thanksgiving feast while we sit on the lanai and watch the sunset." She kicked her shoes off, slipped her T-shirt over her head, and shimmied out of her shorts, revealing a hot pink string bikini. "Bet I can beat you to the ocean," she teased, darting off.

Soon, they were splashing around in the warm water, the sun beating down on them. Jack wrapped his tanned arms around Tess and kissed her. They stared at each other, the energy between them electric.

"I could get lost in your big, brown eyes," he said.

She smiled and said, "Come on, let's dry off." They walked to their pool and lay together on a chaise lounge.

"Jack?" Tess whispered.

"Yeah, baby."

"I know you hold back sometimes, but you don't need to."

"Tess…"

"Baby, I know you do. There's nothing that could ever happen between us that I wouldn't want."

He caressed the side of her face. "You're so beautiful and delicate. I just want you to feel safe and loved."

"I do and I always will."

"You've been through so much. It wasn't that long ago that Ray was stalking you; I know that brought up memories of your childhood abuse. I don't ever want to be the cause of your pain or remind you of the ways you have suffered."

"You couldn't. You only push those thoughts further away. I trust you, Jack. Nothing could ever change that. I want to share everything with you. I've never felt as close to another human being as I do to you." She ran her fingers through his wet, salty hair and said, "I still remember the first time we came here, before we owned this place. You took me in the shower and we were so free."

He grazed his fingers along her cheek.

"I'm gonna rinse off," she said. She untied her bikini top, let it fall to the floor, and headed for the outdoor shower.

Jack hustled out of his swim trunks and followed her. She flipped the water on, turned toward him, and smiled. He cupped her face in his hands, kissed her softly, and with one swift movement, swung her around and pulled her bathing suit bottom down. "Don't let me hurt you," he whispered. He pushed her against the wall and they made love passionately.

With his quivering body pressed tightly against hers, Jack kissed Tess's neck and nibbled on her ear. Finally satiated, he turned the shower off and wrapped towels around each of them. He picked her up and cradled her in his arms as he carried her to a lounge chair. They resumed their tender kisses, Jack caressing the side of her face. He looked at her with unadulterated adoration.

"I love you so much," he said.

"I love you too. More than anything."

***

"Look at the sky. How does the sunset grow more beautiful each day? The pink and coral – it's breathtaking," Tess said, standing on their large veranda overlooking the sea.

Jack stood behind her, wrapped his arms around her, and rested his chin on her shoulder. They stood together in silence for a moment, appreciating the majesty of the technicolor clouds. "Every minute we've spent alone here has been heaven."

"We're so lucky, Jack. We have so much magic in our lives."

He kissed the top of her head. "Come on, let's eat. Your veggie burger and grilled pineapple await. The beauty of our outdoor dining table is that we can still enjoy the view."

He pulled out her chair and she sat down. "I'm impressed; you've become quite the grill master. This is the perfect Thanksgiving dinner. Thank you, baby."

"I'm glad we decided to spend the holiday alone."

"Me too. You know how I've always dreaded holidays. They were torture growing up in my house of horrors. Then, in college, everyone would go home, and Omar and I would be left on our own. I always felt terrible that his family didn't accept him, but I can't imagine how lonely I would have been without him. After my first novel came out, I made a conscious effort to be on the road for every holiday, always in a foreign country on Thanksgiving, where it was just another day. I never dreamed my life would be like this. Everything is different now that I have you. I'm more grateful than I could possibly say. Wherever you are, that's home to me."

"We're family and we always will be. I want to celebrate everything with you. Tess, I love you with my whole heart, forever. Happy Thanksgiving, sweetheart."

CHAPTER 2

Two nights later, they met their friends back at their regular Washington DC haunt, Shelby's Bar. Jack and Tess arrived early to claim their usual table by the dance floor, and Omar and Clay were close behind.

Omar embraced Tess tightly, whispering, "Oh Butterfly, how I've missed you."

"I missed you more," she replied. "Without you, who would mercilessly tease me in a posh British accent?"

They hugged for such a long time that Clay joked that they were causing a scene. Joe, Bobby, and Gina arrived shortly after. They greeted each other jubilantly; it had been two months since they had all been together, so when the first round of drinks arrived, they toasted to their joyful reunion.

An hour later, Tess was nuzzling into Jack, serene expressions painted on their faces.

Omar watched them, smiling. "Well, look at you, my little sun-kissed goddess. It seems that a couple of months in Maui with your man was just what the doctor ordered."

"Everyone should be so lucky. It was exquisite. You'll see for yourself when you and Clay have your honeymoon there," she replied.

"We don't know how to thank you. It's the most wonderful gift," Clay said.

"It's our pleasure. Everyone deserves time in paradise with the one they love," Jack said, squeezing Tess's hand.

Tess smiled. "Gina, thank you again for inviting us to Thanksgiving. It was so sweet of you to think of us. We just decided to do our own private thing and soak up one more sunset."

"Who can blame you? Bobby and I are still recovering from overeating," Gina said. She turned to Bobby. "I still don't know how you ate that massive turkey and stuffing sandwich only an hour after dinner."

"I'm more concerned about surviving your mother's Christmas feast," he said, grabbing a fistful of pretzels. "Guys, Gina's mom goes all out for Christmas with an Italian spread that would put the Corleones to shame. And it's just as scary, too. You eat until you can't stand on your own two feet anymore, and if you don't, I think they might take you out back and shoot you."

Everyone laughed.

"I'm telling you, baked ziti, gnocchi, eggplant parm, chicken parm, meatballs, lasagna, bruschetta, and three or four different soups. I'm like, dude, there's only eight people here," he said with a laugh.

Gina playfully punched his arm. "It's what they're used to."

"Yeah, well I'll be wearing sweatpants and carrying a bottle of antacids in my pocket."

"Gina, Thanksgiving dinner was wonderful. It was so nice of you to include me," Joe said.

"The more the merrier," she replied. "I love the holidays."

"With any luck, I'll be spending this Christmas with a special lady," Joe said.

"Do tell," Tess prodded.

He blushed. "It's too early for details, but I've met an incredible woman."

"That's great," Jack said.

"I'm so happy for you," Tess said.

"I owe you one, Tess. You encouraged me to put myself out there."

"Well, we can't wait to meet her, although you're probably wise to keep her all to yourself. You know how this group gets."

"I know that dig was directed at me," Omar said.

Tess giggled. "Well, there's one in every crowd. We have you."

Omar chucked a pretzel at her. "Butterfly, I'm so glad you and Jack had your romantic holiday, but I must admit that I missed you terribly. We have spent every Thanksgiving and Christmas together for decades, so it hardly feels like the holidays without you."

Tess smiled. "I know. We've certainly had some adventures."

"We sure did. I was telling Clay about our escapades, trying to decide which was the most fun or the most insane. Remember getting kicked out of that taxi in Athens on Christmas?"

"How could I forget?"

"For those of you who have not been to Greece, let me just say that their taxi system leaves a lot to be desired. Bloody hell, it is *not* tourist friendly."

"That's an understatement. But we made up for it in Santorini on New Year's Eve," she replied with a wink.

"We sure did. God, that guy was gorgeous. They don't call them Greek gods for nothing, do they?" he said.

"Excuse me?" Clay said playfully.

"Uh, long time ago, didn't mean to mention it, moving on," Omar said quickly. "So Butterfly, I was thinking that our Thanksgiving in Marrakesh had to have been the best of the bunch. The food was divine, and who would have known you'd be such a good belly dancer? Too bad that skill isn't more useful in daily life."

Tess picked up a pretzel and tossed it at him.

"You know how to belly dance?" Jack asked.

"See what you started?" Tess said, lobbing another pretzel at Omar. "Our hosts treated us to a magnificent vegetarian dinner in my honor, with olives, spiced couscous, a delicious, flaky bread called msemen, chickpea soup, briouats, which are kind of like samosas, some kind of vegetable stew, and so much more. The spread just went on and on. Honestly, it was one of the best meals I've ever eaten."

"You ate all of that?" Jack asked in disbelief.

"I had a bite of everything. Anyway, there were musicians playing wonderful music, and a troupe of beautiful, talented women performed a belly dance. You should have seen their traditional costumes; their bedlah were brightly colored and intricately embroidered, and the gold medallions dangling from their belts caught the light as their hips moved. I was so enthralled that they invited me up and taught me a few moves," Tess said.

"You were disconcertingly good, I must confess," Omar said.

"It was fun."

"So, of the dozens of holidays we spent together, would you say that was your favorite?"

She shook her head.

"Then it must be that Thanksgiving in Brazil; I told Clay about that one too. Those clubs were such fun. It's like no one in that country sleeps at night, bless their hearts. I don't know how you managed to be coherent *and* look fabulous at your book event the next day after dancing all night. Those blokes certainly loved you. Ooh, or was it Thanksgiving in London at Mick's when he threw that wild party and you learned all about the joys of pharmaceuticals?"

Jack raised an eyebrow.

"Don't ask, simple mix up with aspirin, could happen to anyone. We all survived to tell the tale," Omar said.

Tess shook her head. "None of the above. My favorite holiday with you was Christmas, our senior year of college."

"You can't be serious," Omar said, his eyes wide.

She nodded. "It was absolutely my favorite, hands down. Until I met Jack, it was the best holiday I'd ever had."

"Butterfly, we've spent holidays in some of the most spectacular places in the world, being treated like royalty, sometimes by literal royalty, and if not, the American equivalent of movie stars and rock gods. I know you don't place value on fame or glamour, but come on. How could that possibly be your favorite holiday memory?"

"Weren't you happy?" she asked.

"Well, yes. I've never been anything but happy when I'm with you," he replied.

She smiled and Jack rubbed her arm.

"Let me fill everyone in on the story of that Christmas, and then you must tell me how on earth it could possibly be your favorite. So, as always, Tess and I were holiday orphans. Thankfully, we both had on-campus jobs that allowed us to stay in the dorms over break or we would have had nowhere to go. Plus, we were both flat broke, had taken out loans to pay for school, and needed every cent we could get from our crappy, minimum wage jobs to stay afloat. We didn't have a nickel between us. So, like she did every holiday, Tess insisted we go feed the homeless at a shelter. God, we probably spent at least eight hours there, helping with the setup, serving, and cleaning. When we were all done at the shelter, we went back to Tess's room. Thankfully, her psycho roommate had left for the break, and I confess that we did have fun rummaging through her treasure trove of gothic paraphernalia. Do you think she was really a witch, Butterfly?"

Tess giggled. "Definitely."

"We had splurged the day before and picked up a box of macaroni and cheese, that dreadful kind with the gruesome, toxic-looking orange powder, which admittedly was a huge step above the ramen we usually ate. So we made our feast in Tess's pitiful electric cooker, curled up in her bed, and watched *It's A Wonderful Life* on her tiny TV, with commercials, I might add. Neither of us wanted to be alone, so we slept snuggling in Tess's twin bed."

Tess smiled.

"If we had known that Tess was to become a millionaire less than a year later and pay off all our student loans, not to mention grad school for me, something I'm eternally grateful for, perhaps we would have splurged on the canned peas we had considered to go with our meal," Omar said with a laugh.

Jack shifted in his seat and Tess turned to face him. "Before I met Omar, you told me how much he had done for you, but you never told me that you paid for his education."

"Of course I did. He's my family. There's no reason to talk about it," Tess said.

Jack kissed her lightly and tucked a strand of hair behind her ear.

"I should add that when she paid off our student debt, she had no idea of the fortune she was soon to amass. She probably thought it was all the big money she was ever going to earn, and she used every cent of it without a second thought. I was too young to realize how extraordinary that was," Omar said.

Jack put his arm around her. "I can't believe you never told me that."

She shrugged.

"Butterfly, why on earth was that your favorite holiday?"

"Because it was the last holiday before everyone changed, well, everyone but you. It was real."

"There's one other person who never changed, Butterfly, and that's you. Your reality may be a series of life's greatest hits, but it's still your reality. It's always been real because you've been at the center. You've never allowed anyone to take that from you. That's one of the many things I respect the hell out of you for. And none of it fell in your lap. I was there; I remember how bloody hard you worked and how much you sacrificed."

"You don't miss those simple days at all?" Tess asked.

"Sometimes I miss having you all to myself, before I had to share you with the whole planet. But no, I sure as hell don't miss the sound of my stomach growling while I lay awake wondering how I was going to survive and where I belonged. You had all the same challenges, but none of the fear. How'd you pull that off, anyway?"

She let out a huff. "I just didn't know any other way to be."

Omar smiled. "Well, that's enough of a look down memory lane. I say we think ahead. How would you and Jack feel about spending July fourth with us in Venice? We can take them to the casino where that baron taught you to play blackjack, and then we can hit that topless beach you loved."

"You went to a topless beach?" Jack asked in disbelief.

Tess picked up a pretzel and flung it at Omar's head. "See what you started?"

CHAPTER 3

"Butterfly, these cookies are scrumptious. Let me guess, you made them at the White House with your BFF Kate, also known as the president," Omar said, taking another bite.

"You'll always be my BFF. No need to be insecure; it's very unbecoming," Tess replied with a giggle. "But yes, I stopped by Kate's yesterday. With everything that woman has, she didn't own a pizzelle press, so I brought her one as a gift and we broke it in. They're so festive for this time of year. Don't you think they look like snowflakes?"

"They do, but now I look a mess with powdered sugar all over me."

"I suspect Clay won't mind if you come home with a little something sweet on your lips."

"No, I don't suppose he will. Have I thanked you and Jack yet for throwing our wedding? It's beyond generous, and it's going to be fab," Omar said.

"Nonsense, it's our absolute pleasure," Tess replied. "We just need to go over a few final details. Your every wish shall be my command. I have a checklist so we don't forget anything."

Omar smiled.

"Are you sure you want to keep the guest list so small? Just our group?"

"I'm certain. Clay and I have talked about it quite a bit, and we decided that since our relatives can't come, we don't need a slew of casual friends and acquaintances, just those that matter the most. We really just want our family and very closest friends. That's you, Jack, Joe, Bobby, and Gina."

"Well, it will be fantastic. Jack and I are sending the jet to fly all of you to Maui. You'll have a day to unwind, then we've planned a ceremony on the beach and a luau with incredible food and entertainment, just as you requested. You and Clay will be in a luxurious suite at the Four Seasons so you can have privacy, and the others will stay in our guesthouse. We'll do a casual brunch at our house the day after the wedding."

"It sounds absolutely perfect."

"You and Clay deserve everything you could ever hope for. Jack and I are so excited to host your celebration. Now, we booked you for two weeks at the resort so you can have a proper honeymoon. Was Clay able to get the time off from the hospital?"

Omar nodded. "He's looking forward to relaxing on the beach. And of course, I'm looking forward to tropical cocktails. I do love those little paper umbrellas."

Tess smiled. "You still need to select a cake, so please flip through that folder," she said, pointing. "The flowers are a no-brainer in Hawaii. Any special requests for the reception?"

"You said there will be entertainment; will you be wearing a grass skirt, I hope?"

Tess rolled her eyes. "The best you can hope for is an orchid in my hair."

"Well, at least get us one of those fire eaters. They're amazing. Very hot, in every sense."

They were laughing when the phone rang. "Hold that thought," Tess said, running to answer it.

"Hello?"

"Hello. May I please speak with Jack?" a woman asked.

"I'm sorry, he's not here right now. May I take a message?"

"Is this his wife?"

"Yes, this is Tess."

"Hi, Tess. This is Mary Miller, Jack's mother."

"Oh! Hi, Mrs. Miller," Tess said.

"Please, call me Mary. We're family after all."

"All right, Mary."

"I was calling to invite you and Jack to spend Christmas with us in Pennsylvania, if you don't have other plans. His brother Mikey is coming with his family on the twenty-second, and they'll be leaving the day after Christmas. We were hoping you might do the same. Sara, Jack's sister, will be here with her husband on Christmas Day."

"Oh, that's very generous of you. We don't have plans that I'm aware of."

"We miss Jack so much, more than I can say, and we would all love to meet you," Mary said. "Will you please tell him I called and talk it over?"

"Of course. I promise you'll hear from him soon," Tess replied.

"It was lovely speaking with you. I'll be waiting for Jack's call. Goodbye," Mary said.

"Goodbye."

"Who was that, Butterfly?" Omar asked, wiping powdered sugar from his lips.

"Jack's mother. She invited us to spend Christmas with them in Pennsylvania."

"I didn't even know Jack had a mother."

Tess raised an eyebrow.

"You know what I mean. He didn't have any relatives at your wedding and I've never heard him mention his family."

"Yeah, he never talks about them. He told me a little about them when we first got together, but that's it."

"Well, what did he say?"

"Only good things. They were close. Sounded very all-American, pretty religious, which Jack isn't. He lost touch with them. When he joined the Bureau, he was in the field doing extremely dangerous work, deep undercover stuff for many years. I think he was trying to protect them. I know he expected to be killed in the line of duty, and I think he didn't want them to worry. He lied and gave them the impression that he had an office job with the FBI. Didn't want them to know what it was really like or that he worked in counterterrorism. I don't think he's spoken to them in more than a decade, maybe two."

"Wow. Well, do you think you'll go to Christmas?" Omar asked.

Tess shrugged. "Honestly, I have no idea how he'll react. I think we should go. He deserves to have his family."

"So strange, how these things unfold. I guess that planning the wedding has me thinking about who really matters in our lives and who doesn't. Clay was close to his parents, but his father is dead and his mother is in a care facility, unaware of who she is, let alone who he is. My family wants nothing to do with me simply because of who I love. Even though it's been decades, I still miss them. Your family was a violent nightmare. And now, Jack has a family that bloody well may be that kind that we all long for, and he may not want to see them."

"You got one thing wrong there. *We* are family. Those people who hurt us were just relatives," Tess said.

Omar smiled. "Indeed, Butterfly. Sounds like Jack's relatives were more of the family variety."

Tess nodded. "Yeah, I think so."

***

"Hi, sweetheart. These are for you," Jack said, handing Tess a bouquet of white hydrangeas.

"Thank you. They're beautiful," she said, taking the flowers and kissing him. "What's the occasion?"

"I love you, that's all."

She smiled. "Did you have a good lunch with Joe?"

"Yeah. He's crazy about the woman he's seeing, Luciana. I've never seen him like this before. He said he's having the time of his life. She even makes him go dancing at a bar that plays salsa music or something. That's how you know a man is in deep, when he'll do things he never would have done before."

"Is that how you knew with me?"

He stroked her cheek with the back of his hand, kissed her, and said, "Sweetheart, I knew the first night we met that I wanted to spend the rest of my life with you. I was putty in your hands."

She looked down, blushing, and he kissed the top of her head.

"Well, I can't wait to meet Luciana. I know Joe's been lonely for a long time," Tess said.

"Do you think Omar and Clay would mind if he brought her to Maui for the wedding?"

"Of course not."

"How's Omar? Did you two finish up the wedding planning?"

"He's great. Honestly, he's so happy that he's basically letting us take care of all the arrangements. I don't think he cares about anything except being with Clay. They're perfect for each other;

14

I'm glad they're finally making it official. It's hard to explain unless you're like he and I are, but when you don't have relatives in your life, it means so much to know that someone loves you and will always be there. Like how I feel about you," she said, resting her hand on his.

"Sweetheart, you're stuck with me for life. I'm your family and I always be."

She smiled. "Jack, I need to talk to you about something. Let's sit in the living room." They sat down on the couch and Tess took Jack's hand. "Honey, your mother called."

"What? Is everything okay?"

"Yes, they're fine. She called to invite us to Christmas."

He sat silently with a lost look in his eyes.

"Your brother and his family are going. They're staying for four nights, which is what your mother would like us to do. Your sister is coming for Christmas Day. I promised your mother we'd talk about it and that you'd call her back."

"Tess, I haven't seen them in over fifteen years."

She put her hand on his cheek. "They miss you."

"I doubt my father misses me. He thinks I'm a piece of shit."

"I find it hard to believe anyone could ever think that about you."

"Trust me, he does. He thinks I abandoned my family. From his point of view, he's right."

"He's not right. He doesn't know what you were doing all those years, how brave and selfless you are," she said.

"The ironic thing is that I always wanted to be like him. He was in the military, and after that, he became a firefighter. He spent his life trying to protect people."

"Sounds like someone I know," she said.

"He's retired now. They don't know it, but I keep tabs on them. He always told us to put family, community, and country first. It's why I enlisted. When I joined the Bureau, the path I took was just too dark. It didn't leave room for family, and I was afraid of putting them at risk, making them a target. At first, I tried to go home once a year, sent holiday cards, called once in a blue moon. But it was just too hard. I felt they were better off without me, so I let them go for their sake. They have no idea why. My father thinks I sat behind a desk for twenty years. Little does he know that I was a field agent doing deep undercover work. I was only trying to protect them."

"Well, this is your chance to reconnect, to tell him the truth. Your life is simpler now; maybe this is the time. Do you miss them?"

"I don't let myself think about it. Before I met you, I blocked out all of my feelings. That was the only way to do my job, to do the unspeakable things that were required, to live that kind of life. My life was dedicated to a mission, to my country, not my own happiness. I didn't allow myself to feel or have any relationships."

"Jack, you're the most caring person I've ever met, and your life is completely different now. You have a chance to love each other again."

He became misty. "Tess, they don't even know about Gracie. How could I possibly tell them they had a grandchild who died, who they never even got to meet?"

"You either decide to tell them so they can get to know you better, or you don't; that's your choice. But Jack, you have a family who obviously loves you. They're reaching out. Your mother sounded really nice."

"She is," he said softly.

"Were you close with your siblings?"

He nodded. "Mikey is a year younger. He was basically my best friend. His wife Julie was his high school sweetheart, so I've known her forever. She's a doll. My sister Sara is five years younger. She was always a good kid. She's married, but I've never met her husband."

"Well then, don't miss this opportunity."

"I can't ask you to do this, Tess. You don't even know them."

"Jack, I'd be thrilled to go. I'll get to know them in no time. Honestly, after your mother called, I felt terrible. I don't have a childhood family or any relatives I speak to. Neither does Omar. I guess that's why I never pushed you to talk more about your family; I just didn't even know to do that. I'm sorry. I want you to have every good thing in this life. Please don't use me as a reason not to reconnect. I'll go anywhere with you. We can take the jet and then rent a car."

He sniffled and said, "You have no idea how much I love you."

"Yes, I do. As much as I love you. Go call your mother. I got the feeling she was going to be waiting by the phone."

He put his hand on the back of her head and pulled her toward him, kissing her softly. She smiled and he got up to make the call.

***

"A shopping mall has to be the worst place to be before Christmas," Jack said as they entered the building.

"Oh, come on, circling the lot for twenty minutes, narrowly missing two collisions, and that guy giving us the finger – what says 'holiday spirit' more?" Tess asked with a laugh.

Jack smiled faintly.

"Ooh, let's grab a seat on that bench and make a game plan."

"It's a zoo here," Jack said, taking a seat.

"Yeah, I forgot what malls are like. I guess this is what we get for putting our shopping off until a week before Christmas. I can only imagine the line at gift wrapping. Okay, I've got the list. I know Mikey's twin boys are eight, so I researched what kids like at that age, and there's a cool video game that's the hot gift this year. We can start there," Tess said.

"Sweetheart, we really don't have to do this. You can just have your assistant get things for them or we can buy gift cards online."

"First of all, Crystal isn't that kind of assistant. Second, gift cards? Really, Jack? What could be more impersonal? Let's try to get them thoughtful gifts they'll actually enjoy."

"I don't want you to feel like you have to waste your time on this."

"Buying gifts for people you love is hardly a waste of time. I can't think of a better way to spend the day. Besides, we're together and that's all that matters. We'll start with the boys, but then you need to tell me about everyone else so we know what to get."

"I wouldn't know where to begin. I really don't know them anymore, Tess."

"Yes, you do. What does your mother like?"

"She loves reading. She's a retired librarian, so you two will have a lot in common."

17

Tess smiled.

"She also loves cooking and baking, especially around the holidays."

"Well, that's easy then. What about your father? God, I just realized I don't even know his name."

"John," Jack replied.

"You were named after him?"

"Yeah," he muttered.

"We'll start with the kids and your mother. You can spend some time thinking about everyone else. Come on, I think the electronics are this way," Tess said, pulling his hand.

"Wait."

"Yeah, baby?" She looked into his sea-colored eyes with reassurance and love.

He gently brushed the hair from the side of her face and said, "Thank you."

She smiled. "If you behave, we can even get one of those oddly large cinnamon rolls you like, and I may even model some lingerie for you."

He laughed.

CHAPTER 4

Jack parked in front of the house. "This is it." Tess examined the yellow colonial house with its snow-covered lawn and wreath hanging on the front door. She smiled. Jack leaned over and kissed her. "Thank you for doing this."

"I'm happy to," she replied.

"I'll grab the luggage and come back for the gifts," Jack said.

"I've got the flowers," Tess said, holding the large red and white bouquet.

They started up the walkway and the door swung open. An older woman with Jack's eyes stood beaming.

"Hi, Mom," Jack said. "Let me put these down." He walked into the doorway, put the bags down, and his mother hugged him tightly.

"I missed you. We're so glad you're here," she said, tears in her eyes.

"Missed you too," Jack whispered. He turned to his father. "Hi, Dad."

"Well, come on in," his father replied, stepping back.

"You must be Tess," Mary said. "You're such a tiny thing in person. Isn't she small in person, John? People always look bigger on television and in magazines, I guess."

Tess smiled. "It's nice to meet you. Thank you for having us. These are for you."

"Our pleasure, dear. We're so glad to finally meet you," Mary said, hugging her. "These are gorgeous, thank you," she said, taking the flowers.

"Hi, Tess. Welcome," John said, extending his hand. She leaned in and gave him a gentle hug.

"Uh, I'll help Jack with the luggage," John grumbled.

"That's okay, Dad. I got it. I'm just going to grab the gifts."

Jack ran outside and Mary turned to Tess. "May I take your coat?"

"Thank you," Tess replied, handing it to her.

Jack returned a moment later, his arms overflowing. "I'll stick these under the tree."

Tess followed him into the living room. There was a large Christmas tree in the corner, encircled by ribbons of white twinkly lights and topped with a shimmering star. The whole house smelled of pine. Tess smiled and said, "It's so pretty."

"The boys will decorate it tonight. We always leave the ornaments and tinsel for them. They just love it. But we have to put the star up before they get here or they'll fight over it," Mary said.

"Mikey and Julie aren't here yet?" Jack asked.

"Their flight was delayed. Lots of holiday headaches with the airlines reported on the news," John said. "How about you guys, any problems?"

"We flew private, Dad. Tess has a jet."

"Oh, uh, I see," John mumbled.

"Well, let me show you to your room. Once you're all settled, we can have a cup of tea or some coffee," Mary said.

"We can manage, Mom. Are we in my old room?"

"No, we put you in Sara's old room because we upgraded it to a queen-size bed and it has a private bathroom," Mary replied. She turned to Tess. "I hope it's all right."

Tess smiled. "I'm sure it's perfect."

Jack picked up their bags and Tess followed him upstairs. They walked into the guestroom, which had been tidied and decorated with care; fresh, folded towels waited on the bed, and flowers in a bud vase adorned the nightstand. Jack shut the door, dropped the luggage, and grabbed Tess. He started kissing her fervently. "Baby, what are you doing?" she whispered.

"I just feel compelled," he said, his hands on her waist.

She kissed him softly and said, "Come on. Let's unpack and go spend time with your parents."

***

Tess and Jack joined his parents in the living room. They were each sitting in a reclining chair, so Jack and Tess plopped down on the couch. "Would you prefer tea or coffee?" Mary asked.

"Either is fine, thank you. Whatever you're having," Tess said.

"Same," Jack said.

"John, please help me," Mary said.

"Do you need a hand?" Tess asked, standing up.

"You're our guest. Please make yourself comfortable," Mary replied.

Tess sat and Jack slung his arm around her.

"Is it strange being back?" she asked.

He nodded. "They've aged more than I had imagined. It shows me just how much I've missed. I can see that my father isn't happy I'm here."

"Just give it a chance," she urged.

John returned with a teapot and four cups. "I've got it, Dad," Jack said, leaning forward to pour everyone's tea. John went back to the kitchen and returned again with small plates, forks, and napkins. Mary followed, holding a crystal tray with a round cake slathered in chocolate frosting.

"It's my marble cake. I only make it for special occasions," she said.

"Tess doesn't eat cake," Jack said.

Tess looked at her husband with an expression of horror. She turned to Mary. "I'd love a small piece, please. It looks delicious."

John started slicing the cake.

"Oh, before I forget…" Mary ran off without completing her thought. She returned a moment later with a stack of Tess's books, all lovingly tattered. She placed them on the coffee table with a pen. "I'm an avid reader and I used to be a librarian."

"Jack told me," Tess said.

"You've done so much for libraries and literacy in this country. I've admired you for many years," Mary said.

Tess smiled. "Thank you. Libraries are very special to me. I have great respect for librarians; thank you for all that you've done."

"You're one of my favorite authors. I always recommended your books. They're so beautiful and inspirational. I don't know how you manage to write so poignantly about the human condition with all its complexity. There's a rawness to your writing, something that hits far beneath the surface. I can't quite name it, but it touches people deeply."

"That's very kind," Tess said.

"I know some reviewers say they're full of pain. Uh, 'the people's high priestess of pain,' I believe they've called you."

"Yeah."

"I think they're full of hope. They should really call you 'the pied piper of hope,'" Mary said.

Tess smiled.

"I was hoping you'd sign these for me," Mary said, pushing the books closer to Tess.

"Of course. It would be my pleasure."

"When I read your last novel and saw that it was dedicated to my Jack, I just couldn't believe it," Mary said. "I told all my friends."

"Well, I love Jack very much. I couldn't have written it without him."

Mary and John exchanged looks.

"Are you working on a new novel?" Mary asked.

Tess shook her head. "The last two came out so close together, and the most recent one took a lot out of me. I've written a couple of essays influenced by our travels, but I'm waiting for inspiration to strike for my next novel."

"I retired years ago, but I still help with events at the library from time to time. Mostly local authors and that kind of thing. I was thinking that the day after Christmas, before you leave, you might want to come and do a reading. It would be such a treat for the town. We've never had anyone like you here before."

"Mom, Tess doesn't want to work," Jack said.

Tess looked at Jack with a bewildered expression.

"Uh, I would be happy to do that, Mary," Tess said.

"I don't want to trouble you. It was just an idea," Mary said, sheepishly.

John handed them each a slice of cake and they started eating.

"So Jack, you still sitting behind a desk at the Bureau?" John asked.

"No. I left about a year ago. We wanted to travel and we bought a place in Hawaii. We go back and forth between Maui and DC. Tess has a place in LA too, so sometimes we spend a little time there," Jack said.

"So your wife supports you?" John asked.

"Dad, I still do consulting work."

"Really, the money isn't an issue. I've done very well," Tess said. "We just wanted to enjoy our lives and spend as much time together as possible."

"Yes, I see. I read you're worth over half a billion dollars. Is that true? Don't mean to pry, but it is public knowledge," John said.

"Something like that," Tess said.

"It's obviously very impressive what you've done with your life. I know you're hardworking and self-made, which I respect. Of course, there are some people who think the accumulation of personal wealth is immoral," John said.

"Dad," Jack cautioned.

"It's fine," Tess said, rubbing Jack's knee. "John, I don't disagree with you. That's why I give most of what I earn to charity. I keep a large base to invest and grow interest, which allows me to donate to causes that are important to me, and to Jack."

"I told you that, John," Mary said. She turned to Tess. "I've read all about you and seen you interviewed on television many times."

"Yeah, I'm sorry. It's very commendable. How long have you two been married?" John asked.

"Three years," Jack said.

"How'd you wind up with my son?" John asked.

"Just luck, I guess," Tess said, taking Jack's hand.

"You didn't want kids, Tess?" John asked.

"Dad!"

"Well, it's just that you've never been family oriented, didn't put family first like your siblings. I was only curious if that was an issue for Tess," John said.

Tess put her hand on Jack's thigh. "We decided to focus on our relationship, that's all," Tess said. "Me and Jack, we're family."

Jack covered Tess's hand with his own.

"Sorry, didn't mean anything by it. You should see Mikey with his twin boys, they're eight now; I guess your mother probably told you that. Mikey's a real family man. He and Julie had a huge wedding right here at our church. They lived nearby until a couple years ago when Julie got a job at a big hospital in Chicago. And Sara, she's six months pregnant, did you know that?" John asked.

"Yeah, Mom told me on the phone," Jack replied.

"She's having a little girl," Mary said. "We're so excited for our first granddaughter. We can't wait to spoil her with pink and purple everything."

Jack looked down.

"Tess, are you close with your family?" John asked.

"Dad, enough with the third degree," Jack snapped.

"It's fine, honey," Tess said, rubbing Jack's leg. "It's a normal thing to ask." She turned to John and Mary. "My parents are dead. I don't have any family to speak of, not in the way you mean. We were never close. I wish we could have been."

Just then, the doorbell rang. "Ah, your brother's here," John said.

John and Mary got up to answer the door.

Tess leaned over and whispered in Jack's ear, "Are you okay?"

"I'm fine."

***

The kids finished trimming the tree while Mary and John set the dining room table. Tess, Jack, Mikey, and Julie were chatting in the kitchen.

"I really missed you, Jack," Mikey said.

"I missed you too. I feel like I should explain," Jack replied.

Mikey shook his head. "You don't have to. To be honest, I was angry at you for a long time. Hurt, really. But I know you. You must have had your reasons. Let's leave it in the past."

"Thanks," Jack said. "I'm glad we have this time together and that you can get to know Tess."

"Damn, she's smokin'," Mikey said.

"She can hear you," Jack replied.

"Don't worry, she doesn't mind," Tess said with a giggle.

"Jack always got the hotties in school. They just loved his quiet, tough-guy thing," Mikey said.

"Mikey, you're not helping," Jack said.

"Oh, I think he's doing fine. I'm looking forward to lots of embarrassing stories," Tess said.

"You're out of luck. Jack was always too cool to do embarrassing things," Julie said.

"Well, that's disappointing," Tess replied.

Mary called, "Okay everyone, dinner is served."

They all sat down. "Would you like some wine or a beer?" Mary asked Tess.

"No, thank you. Just some water, please. I don't drink."

"Are you an alcoholic, dear? I know a lot of celebrities go to that Betty Ford Center. I hear it's very good," Mary said.

"No, I'm not an alcoholic, I just don't drink. Really, I'm not even a celebrity. Just a writer who's had a bit of luck."

"I hope dinner is okay," Mary said. "Jack told me you're a vegetarian. We've never had one of those here. I read you lived in Los Angeles for a long time, and I hear everyone is on a crazy diet there."

"Everything looks great, thank you," Tess said.

John cleared this throat and said, "We thank the Lord for this bounty and all the blessings bestowed upon this family. Amen."

"Well, everybody, help yourselves," Mary said.

They all began eating. Halfway through their meal, Mary turned to Tess and said, "We made a reservation for tomorrow night. It's so nice that you and Jack wanted to take everyone out."

"Our pleasure. It's so kind of you to host all of us," Tess replied.

"On Christmas Eve, we'll have dinner at five and then go to church. It's wonderful; there's a choir I look forward to hearing every year. Really puts you in the holiday spirit," Mary said.

"Mom, Tess is Jewish, and actually, she's atheist, so she doesn't want to go to church," Jack said.

Tess looked at him and furrowed her brow. "Actually, I've been to services with my friends at mosques, temples, and all kinds of churches all around the world. I'd be happy to go with you."

Everyone smiled awkwardly.

Mary forged ahead, past the discomfort. "On Christmas Day, we eat at three. It's our tradition. I'll do all the baking tomorrow morning. I make loads of Christmas cookies from scratch; everyone has a different favorite. Then, I do the cooking on Christmas Eve and Christmas morning. When Sara's here, she helps. They only live forty minutes away, but they're spending Christmas Eve with her in-laws, so they'll be here midday on Christmas. Julie's not much for cooking."

"No, I'm not," Julie said. "You'd all end up in the hospital if you ate anything I made. Luckily, I'm a nurse and Mikey's an EMT, so you're covered if I give you food poisoning," she said with a laugh.

Tess giggled.

"Do you cook, dear? I hear that most celebrities have private chefs or they order from one of those fancy food delivery things. I can't imagine not picking out my own groceries," Mary said.

"Actually, I'd be happy to help you. I love to cook. I do all of our grocery shopping and cooking, and Jack often helps. Really, our lives are much simpler than you might imagine. Once we get to know each other, I'm sure you'll see we have a lot in common."

Mary smiled.

"When we're in DC, I have a good friend who I get together with every couple of weeks just to bake cookies or muffins or whatever. Kate, my friend, has a highly stressful job, and baking is the only way she can relax."

"That's nice," Mary said. "What does your friend do?"

"Well, she's the president," Tess replied matter-of-factly.

"The president of what, dear?" Mary asked.

"The United States." Tess picked up her fork to take a bite of noodle casserole.

Everyone looked at one another, their mouths agape. Jack put his hand on Tess's back.

"She's just a regular person, like anyone else, who happens to have an irregular job. She's a wonderful baker," Tess said. "She has a lot of old family recipes. I've learned some great tricks baking with her."

"Uh... well okay then, you can help me with the cookies tomorrow morning," Mary said.

Tess smiled. "Great."

***

When Tess and Jack got back to their room, they each took a turn washing up in the bathroom. Jack came out and saw Tess standing in black lace underwear and her bra, about to put her pajamas on. He grabbed her and ran his hands down her body.

"Baby, I was just going to put my pajamas on."

"Be with me, Tess," he said, kissing her neck.

"Jack, it's your parents' house."

"So what? We're married."

"Jack, it isn't right."

"Just come lie with me like this. You look so pretty. Just let me kiss you." He took her hand and led her to the bed, laying down and pulling her on top of him. He put his hands in her hair and they started kissing passionately. Gingerly, he unhooked her bra.

"Jack, that's not just kissing," she whispered.

He rolled her onto the bed, tossed her bra aside, and put one hand under her head, tenderly caressing the side of her breast with his fingertips. "You're so beautiful, Tess, inside and out," he whispered, staring at her. "Be with me. I need to feel you. Please, baby."

"Okay, Jack. I always want you," she whispered.

"Tell me you're mine."

"You know I'm yours. Always," she said, looking into his warm, blue eyes.

He kissed her softly. They made love, trying to muffle any noise. After, they lay side by side, Jack running his fingers through her hair.

"I love you so much, Tess. You mean everything to me."

"I love you too," she said, tracing the scars on his shoulder.

"Let's sleep like this, with you in my arms," he said.

She nodded and rested her head on his chest. He wrapped his arms around her and they fell asleep.

CHAPTER 5

Tess woke up and turned to face Jack. He was lying on his back, already wide awake. She put her hand on his stomach and whispered, "Good morning, baby."

"Good morning," he said, and he pulled her on top of him.

"Jack, I need to brush my teeth and we're not having sex again."

"But it was so good to feel you, to be with you last night," he said, running his hands down her body.

"No way, Jack. You'll just have to control yourself," she said with a smile.

"Okay, let me look at you before you cover this work of art in clothing," he said, putting his hands in her hair.

"This is why we should never sleep in the nude."

"It's why we always should."

She rolled off of him and stood up. "Geesh, it's cold. I need to hop in the shower. I promised your mother I'd help her with the Christmas cookies this morning."

"Come for a run with me," he said.

"I can't. I'm going to help your mother. You can go if you want," she said, darting into the bathroom.

Jack heard the sink turn on and then off. When he heard the shower running, he got up and opened the bathroom door. He peeked behind the shower curtain.

"Oh my God. You startled me," Tess said.

"Room for two in there?"

She nodded.

He stepped in and put his hands on her hips. "I'm not done with you," he said, kissing her neck.

"You're incorrigible and I don't know what's gotten into you. But you are the sexiest man on this planet, and I can't resist."

***

Tess was at the counter dusting snowflake cookies with powdered sugar, the boys were at the table frosting shortbread cookies, and Mary was pulling gingersnaps out of the oven when Jack came into the kitchen.

"Hi, honey," Tess said. "Mikey and Julie went to visit an old friend. We're watching the boys."

"Looks and smells like a bakery in here," Jack said.

"The chocolate chips are cool. They're over there," Tess said, tilting her chin.

"Are those still your favorite, Jack?" Mary asked.

"Yeah," he replied.

Mary cheerily said, "Tess taught me a wonderful trick she learned from her friend Kate, I mean the president, I mean, well, you know. Anyway, they're even better than my old recipe."

"Try a cookie," Tess said. "There's fresh coffee too."

Jack poured a cup of coffee and took a cookie. He sat at the table with the boys. John walked into the room.

"Sit down and have a cookie and some coffee with Jack," Mary said.

John got a cup of coffee and sat at the table. "Those look good," he said to the boys.

"They're having a grand old time," Mary said. "They're great helpers, although we'll be cleaning up for ages. Boys are the messiest. I can't wait to have a little grandbaby girl around here."

"You're gonna give the boys a complex," John said.

Mary smirked.

John turned to Jack. "Your mother is so excited for her first granddaughter. Talks about it nonstop. She buys everything pink she sees."

Tess glanced at Jack and he looked down. He inhaled deeply and said, "Dad, Mom, there's something I have to tell you. There's no easy way. I had a daughter."

Mary's jaw hit the floor. She hastily cleaned her hands with a dish towel and scurried over to Jack. "What? How could you keep this from us?"

"I didn't know her. She wasn't in my life."

"Are you saying you abandoned her?" John asked.

"I didn't know about her. Her mother never told me," Jack said.

"I don't understand. How didn't you know?" Mary asked.

"Mom, she was a woman I met one night in a bar. I didn't see her after that."

"Is that how you conduct yourself?" John bellowed.

Before Jack could respond, Mary said, "Had? You said had."

"When she was four years old, her mother contacted me. She was sick, Mom," he said with tears in his eyes. "She had leukemia. She died. It's been about four years since I lost her. I didn't tell you because I didn't want you to experience the kind of pain I felt. But being here, listening to you go on and on about your first granddaughter, I just…"

"Jack, how could you do this? How could you get a woman pregnant and then not be in the child's life? You never did put family first," John said, shaking his head in disappointment.

"I'm sorry you feel that way," Jack said, and he pushed back from the table and left the room.

John and Mary just looked at each other in silence.

Tess took a deep breath and gently said, "I can only imagine how stunned you are, it's a lot to take in, but the mother never told Jack he had a child. He didn't know. When he found out, he rushed to the hospital. He begged the doctors to take his bone marrow, but it was too late. He spent eleven days and nights there by his daughter's side until she died, even though she didn't know who he was. That's the kind of man he is; he would have traded his life for hers in a heartbeat. He thinks about her every day. Her death has caused him tremendous heartache."

Mary and John looked unable to formulate words, unable to make sense of this new information.

"And it might not mean anything to you, but Jack is my family and he has put me first since the day we met. He's taken care of me in every conceivable way. He's a good man. I'm sorry, Mary, but I really should go check on him," Tess said, untying her apron.

As she was leaving the kitchen, Mary called out, "What was her name, Jack's daughter?"

"Gracie."

***

Tess walked into their room to find Jack in running clothes, tying his shoelaces. "Honey," she said, putting her hand on his shoulder. "I'm so sorry. I know your father's reaction was harsh, but honestly, I think they were just in shock."

"It's fine. I know what he thinks of me. It's never going to change."

"Jack, he doesn't know the real you because you haven't been honest with him. I mean, the man thinks you sat behind a desk for the last twenty years and just didn't bother to call or visit. I actually think they've tried to be pretty gracious considering the situation and how little they know."

"You saw how it went when I told them about Gracie."

"Jack, like I said, you dropped a bombshell. They were in shock and responded poorly. And the stuff he said about the one-night stand, he doesn't know that was all you were able to do because of your job. He's passing judgment based on highly limited information."

Jack stood up and avoided Tess's eyes. "I know you mean well, but just leave it alone. I'm going for a run."

"You went for a run this morning," she said.

"I'm going for another one and then a long, hot shower."

He trotted downstairs and Tess followed. As he passed the kitchen, his father called to him. "Jack, your mother and I are terribly sorry about your daughter, about Gracie."

"Thanks," he muttered, and he left the house.

***

That afternoon, the kitchen in the Miller house was bustling with noise. Tess, Julie, and Mikey were making Christmas ornaments with the boys at the table. Mary was washing dishes and John was drying them. Jack came into the room holding his cell phone. "Tess, Omar is on the phone for you. He couldn't reach you on yours."

She looked up, glitter on her face. "I turned the ringer off when we got here. Is everything okay?"

"He said it's a work thing," Jack replied.

"Well, I'm a little busy. Can I call him back?" she asked.

"He said it's urgent but he'll make it quick."

"My hands are a mess. Please set the phone on the table and put it on speaker." She looked at the boys and said, "I'm sorry, this will only take a minute."

Mary turned off the faucet so Tess would have quiet for her call, and Julie put a finger to her lips to hush the boys.

"Hi, Omar. You're on speakerphone. I have glue all over my hands," she said.

"Of course you do," Omar said with a laugh.

"I'm making Christmas ornaments with my nephews."

"Butterfly, Crystal and I have been trying to get in touch with you since yesterday. I need your final approval on the streaming deal for the limited series."

"I turned my phone off. I told you, no work until after the holidays."

"I know and I'm sorry, but they want the write-off on the books for this calendar year. Everyone will be out of the office from tomorrow until after the new year, so we have to get it done today. I know this donation is important to you. I can sign the paperwork; I just need the green light."

She sighed. "Fine."

"You were right," Omar said. "We were able to get them up to three point four million, and they'll make the donations directly. Is it a deal?"

"Yes, that's fine," Tess replied.

"I also need to confirm that you want to donate one hundred percent. Barry's still hoping you'll have a change of heart and keep some of it, but you know how accountants are."

"Well, he can keep hoping. Have them donate the whole thing."

"You still want half to go to veterans and half to that children's wish organization?" Omar asked.

"Yes," Tess replied. "Is that it?"

"I'm afraid there's one last question, and I'm bracing myself for your response. Don't kill the messenger, Butterfly, but your publisher wanted me to ask if you'd reconsider your insistence on keeping the donation anonymous. They'd love to get some publicity out of it. Eliza Elkington could do a profile in her magazine, or you could do a TV spot with Diane."

"Absolutely not. That offends me to the core. You can tell Claire that if I see anything in the media about this, even so much as a whisper, I'll assume they leaked the story and I'll be publishing my next book with someone else."

"I'm sorry, I had to ask."

"Please wish everyone happy holidays and tell Claire I hope her son has recovered well from his injury. Are we done?"

"Yes, Butterfly. I'm sorry to disturb you. I hope you and Jack are having a good trip."

"I love you to pieces, but if you call me about work again, you're fired."

"From your business or your life?"

"Both."

Omar laughed. "If it's any consolation, Butterfly, you're doing a good thing that will help a lot of people."

"Nice attempt at redemption. I'll talk to you when we're back in DC. Give my love to Clay."

She gestured at Jack to hang up. There was complete silence in the room. Mikey and Julie looked up at Jack, their mouths agape. John and Mary looked at each other with shocked expressions and then back at Jack and Tess.

Noticing everyone staring, Tess softly said, "I'm sorry for the interruption."

John cleared his throat. "Tess, I'm a vet."

Tess smiled kindly. "I know. Jack told me. Your service was what inspired him to enlist. Since leaving his full-time job with the Bureau, he's done a lot of wonderful volunteer work to support vets."

John looked at Jack and then at Mary.

"What John's trying to say is that was a very generous thing you did," Mary said.

Tess smiled and turned to the boys. "So, I think the snowflake needs more silver glitter. What do you think? Maybe we can convince your Uncle Jack to sit down and help." She picked up an ornament and began sprinkling sparkling flakes on it. Jack sat down next to her and squeezed her thigh. Mikey looked at him and smiled. Jack craned his neck to look at his parents, and they smiled too. Mary turned the faucet on and went back to washing the dishes. Jack leaned over and kissed Tess on the cheek. "Here," she said, handing him a star ornament. "Why don't you start with this one?"

***

When they arrived at the restaurant, the host greeted them jubilantly and escorted them to a round table in the center of the dining room.

"Do you have anything more private?" Jack asked.

"Honey, we don't want to be stuffed in a corner," Mary said. "This table is perfect."

Jack looked at Tess. "This is great," she said softly. "Let's sit."

"Yeah, okay," he muttered.

They sat down and the host handed them each a menu.

Mary turned to Tess. "It was so nice of you and Jack to take everyone out tonight."

"It's our pleasure. We thought you deserved a night off from cooking," Tess said.

"This is our favorite restaurant," Mary said. "I hope you like it."

"The fried goat cheese salad is to die for," Julie said.

Tess smiled. "I love all the decorations."

"They always do it up nicely for the holidays," Mary replied.

They ordered their meals and continued drinking and reminiscing. Soon, the salad plates were being cleared. The boys were busy drawing in their coloring books, and everyone was chatting cheerfully. Mikey and Julie were telling Tess a hilarious story about sneaking into Jack's prom. She was riveted, but Jack wasn't paying attention. Instead, he was fixated on a large party of women to their right who were staring at Tess. He inadvertently made eye contact with one of the women and she tottered over, wine glass in hand. Jack put his arm protectively around Tess.

"Excuse me," the woman said. "Are you Tess Lee?"

"Yes," Tess replied.

"My girlfriends and I are huge fans. It's taken three bottles of wine for us to have the courage to come over."

Tess smiled. "What's your name?"

"Barbara."

"It's nice to meet you, Barbara."

"We've seen all the movies based on your books. We have a book club and we've read four of your novels so far. My friend Jeanne, over there in the red sweater, was married to a horrible, controlling man. We all knew he was abusive, tried to help her, you know how it goes, but she was stuck. He did a real number on her self-esteem. I suggested we read *Candy Floss* as a group, and she left him after that. I can't tell you how much the book means to her, like a lifeline; she's just too shy to come over."

"That's very sweet," Tess said.

"We just read *Ray of Light* for our last meeting. It was so beautiful and haunting. I cried for days. I still can't stop thinking about the protagonist, wondering if things will work out for her."

"You're very kind," Tess said.

"We hate to bother you during your supper, but would you come over and take a picture with us? My sister isn't here tonight, and she would just die. She's read every one of your books and seen all the shows and movies."

"Sure. I'd be happy to," Tess said. She turned to the table. "Please excuse me."

"I'll take the picture," Jack said, standing up.

They walked over to the table and Tess met each of the women, shaking their hands, hugging them, and listening to their personal stories before taking a slew of photographs, as each woman wanted one on her phone. Eventually, Tess was able to extricate herself, and she and Jack returned to the table. Jack pulled out Tess's chair and she sat down. "I'm so sorry," she said to everyone.

"Don't be. That was so cool," Mikey said.

"Does that happen a lot?" Julie asked.

"Yes," Jack said. "That's why I always try to get a private table, so Tess isn't harassed all night."

"I'm sorry," Mary said in a distressed voice. "I didn't realize."

Tess looked at Jack, horrified. "It's fine, really. I don't mind."

"Those assholes at the bar have been looking at you all night," Jack mumbled, taking a swig of his beer.

"Jack, don't speak that way in front of the kids," Tess said.

"If I see even one of those guys with his phone out to sneak a picture of you, I'm going over there," he said.

"Jack," Tess said softly. She put her hand on his, caressing his fingers. "Relax, honey."

Everyone at the table looked at one another, unsure of what to say or do. The waitress served their entrees and they ate in silence. Tess didn't touch her food.

***

When they were walking to their car after dinner, Jack turned to Mikey and said, "I can't go back to the house right now. How about the four of us go for a drink?"

Mikey called to his mother, "Mom, would you mind taking the boys home and putting them to bed? Julie and I would love to spend a little time with Jack and Tess."

"Sure," Mary replied. "I'll leave a house key under the mat."

"Where to?" Jack asked Mikey.

"That old bar by the barn is still there," Mikey replied.

"We'll meet you there," Jack said.

Jack let Tess into the car and then walked around to the driver's side and got in. "Wait," she said, before he put the key in the ignition. "Can we please talk?"

"About what?"

"Honey, why did you do that? So a few people were looking at me; it wasn't important."

"I know you hate that shit."

"It wasn't a big deal until you turned it into one. You're making your family feel so uncomfortable around me. I don't understand why you did that."

"I'm sorry. I shouldn't have reacted that way. Can we just go get a drink and forget about it?"

"Yeah, okay," she mumbled.

***

The two couples sat in a corner booth at the dimly lit bar and worked on their first round of drinks. Julie said, "They have a jukebox. Want to come pick some songs with me, Tess?"

"Sure," Tess replied.

Tess and Julie headed for the jukebox, and Jack noticed several men staring at them. Tess laughed at something Julie said and she ran her fingers through her hair. Jack couldn't stop watching her or the men blatantly ogling her from their barstools. After a couple of minutes, Tess wandered back alone. "It only takes single dollar bills and I don't have any."

Mikey slipped his hand into his pocket and pulled out three dollar bills.

"Thanks," she said.

Tess returned to the jukebox. When she and Julie turned to head back to the table, a man stopped Tess with a hand on her wrist. Jack tore over. "Hey, she's married," he said forcefully.

"I know, she told me. Sorry," the man said, slinking away.

Tess looked at Jack, furrowing her brow. "He only asked if he could buy me a drink. I said no. It's not a big deal. I thought you were over this kind of thing."

"Yeah, sorry," he mumbled, taking her hand.

They all returned to the table.

"Unsurprisingly, Tess has great taste in music, but you're not going to believe this," Julie said to Mikey. "I picked my go-to song and Tess says, 'Good choice, they're friends of mine,' as if it's nothing. And I'm like, 'Oh my God, what do you mean you're friends?' Well, it turns out that they're really close, so close that Mick was at their super-secret wedding."

Mikey's jaw dropped.

"Before our wedding, we were talking about the guest list, and Tess mentioned that one of her friends is a singer. That's all she said about him," Jack said with a chuckle.

"Well, he is a singer," Tess said with a shrug.

Jack chuckled. "I know, sweetheart."

"Seriously?" Mikey asked.

Jack nodded. "He's a cool guy. Funny. He's mad for Tess. He told me he was curious to meet me because it's rare he meets a man luckier than he is."

Tess rolled her eyes.

"No shit?" Mikey said.

Jack nodded.

"Oh, he's nothing but a big sweetheart," Tess said.

"When he was leaving our wedding, the two of you were whispering to each other, and I couldn't hear any of it. What did he say?" Jack asked.

"Jack…"

"What did he say?" Jack asked again.

Tess looked at him. "He said, 'Darling, you may be the love of my life,' and I said, 'You say that to every woman.' And he said, 'But with you, I mean it.'"

Jack looked at Mikey and Julie, raised his beer bottle, and said, "Told ya."

"Jack, he's just like that. We've been close friends for eighteen years. We have a special connection. We've always understood each other," Tess said.

"Did anything ever happen between you two?" Jack asked.

"Jack, you know we're just friends. You've never cared before. What's gotten into you?"

"Just tell me," Jack said.

"Nothing ever happened," she replied.

"But did he ever try anything?"

"I thought he might the night we met, but I really wasn't sure. I said, 'Let's just have a beautiful friendship,' and he smiled and we've been the best of friends ever since. Okay?"

"I'm sorry, sweetheart. It doesn't matter," he said, leaning over to give her a quick peck. "You never told me how you two met. I'm sure Mikey and Julie would also love to hear."

Mikey and Julie were wide-eyed.

"It was at a party in Paris. I was there with Omar, and Mick showed up with a few friends. Omar and I were trapped in a conversation with the most arrogant, insufferable man, who was trying to impress us with his bank balance. From the corner of my eye, I saw Mick watching us, like he was trying to decide if I needed rescuing. I turned my neck and stuck my tongue out at him. He laughed hysterically, walked over, and asked me to dance. He was trying to save me. After dancing for ages, we sat down with his friends and Omar managed to make his way over. My second novel had just come out, and we were all talking about art and fame. Mick and I bonded over wanderlust and restlessness, something we both knew well. We noticed some people taking pictures of us, and he said something I'll never forget. He said, 'Darling, do you think by chasing freedom, we wound up creating another kind of cage?' I said, 'It doesn't matter. If you're surrounded by light, you won't see the bars.' He smiled, hugged me, and said, 'Where have you been all my life?' We've been friends ever since."

Jack leaned over and kissed her cheek.

"Sara is going to die. She's been in love with him forever. Remember when they did that big tour in the nineties and she begged Mom and Dad for tickets?" Mikey said.

"Well, I can introduce her sometime. It's no problem," Tess said.

"Jack, you did good," Mikey said, raising his beer bottle.

They all smiled.

***

After three more beers, Jack moved on to something stronger. He was downing his third whiskey when Tess touched his arm and said, "Baby, don't you think you've had enough? I've never seen you drink like this."

"It's the holidays. I can hold my liquor," he slurred.

She looked across the table at Mikey and Julie. "I need some air. I'm gonna bum a smoke and go outside for a few minutes."

They nodded.

Jack watched as Tess got up and walked over to the bar. She said something to the bartender, and three men on barstools instantly held out packs of cigarettes. She took one cigarette and the bartender handed her a book of matches. She walked outside, all eyes on her.

"If one of those guys gets up to follow her, I'll beat the hell out of him," Jack said.

"Jack, you've had too much to drink. You need to relax. Stop looking for a fight," Mikey said in a steady voice.

Jack let out a huff. "You haven't spent enough time with Tess. Men go crazy for her."

"I don't think she notices or cares. It's obvious she only has eyes for you," Julie said.

"Look at how they're whispering to each other. They're talking about her," Jack said.

"Ignore it. She does. She's an amazing woman," Julie said.

"She is," Mikey said. "Who wouldn't want to be with a drop-dead beautiful billionaire?"

Julie shot Mikey a look.

"I didn't mean it that way; it's just that she's a catch," Mikey said. "Honestly, we all think she's as sweet as can be, and dude, she's gorgeous. Even if she weren't Tess Lee and she was just some random girl in a bar, I'm sure she could have any guy she wanted."

"That's how we met – in a bar. I had no idea who she was. Fell completely in love with her that night. She's the strongest person I know, but there's also something so sweet, so pure and vulnerable about her. I saw it from the start. I just wanted to be with her, to take care of her, to let her take care of me."

Mikey smiled.

"But I know damn well that you're right. She could have anyone, but it's not because of what she looks like or her net worth. If you spend five minutes with Tess, you just want to be with her forever. You can't imagine her list of admirers. Diplomats, ambassadors for the arts, oil tycoons, even a royal fell for her. Her best friend told me that a bunch of them proposed, too, including a guy from Forbes' wealthiest list, a rock star, but he wouldn't say who." He let out a big huff. "She ended up with me."

"She must love you very much," Julie said.

Jack picked up his glass and gulped the rest of his drink.

When Tess got back to the table, she reported that it was snowing and suggested they leave. She took Jack's keys and drove with Julie. Mikey drove Jack in the other car. When they got to the house, Jack stumbled and knocked over a coatrack in the entryway. Tess righted it and rehung all the coats. She steered him toward their room, where Jack flung off his shoes so hard that they hit the floor with a thud. He stumbled into bed in his clothes. Tess brought him two ibuprofen and a cup of water. "Please take these or you'll get a raging headache."

He swallowed the pills and collapsed onto his pillow. Tess brushed her teeth and slipped into her pajamas. By the time she climbed into bed and turned off the light, Jack was already sound asleep.

CHAPTER 6

Jack woke up, his head throbbing. He pried his eyes open and saw it was after eleven. There was a bottle of ibuprofen and a glass of water on his nightstand with a note that read: *Thought you could use these.* He swallowed a couple, showered, and headed downstairs.

In the kitchen, he found his mother peeling potatoes at the sink. His father, Mikey, and Julie sat at the table, drinking their coffee.

"Good morning," everyone said.

"How are you doing?" Mikey asked.

"I'm fine. Sorry about last night," he mumbled.

"Don't worry about it," Mikey said.

"Yes, we heard you come in. Sounded like you had quite the night," Mary said. "There's coffee, which I assume you need."

"Where's Tess?" Jack asked.

"She's outside with the boys. It snowed all night and they wanted to make a snowman," Julie said.

"Tess is amazing. The boys could stay out there all day; I was out there with them, but once we finished the snowman, I gave up and came in. That was forty-five minutes ago. Tess has been playing and tossing snowballs with them ever since. She's a trooper," Mikey said.

"See for yourself," Mary said, gesturing to the window in front of her. "I've been watching them all morning; they're having a ball. She's so joyful, just pure joy. Poor girl must be frozen to the bone, though, as tiny as she is."

Jack looked out the window. Tess and the boys were lying on the front lawn, making snow angels and laughing hysterically. He stood watching them, a warm smile across his face.

"She's super sweet," Julie said. "I have to confess that I was really nervous about meeting her because she's so successful and all. I didn't know what to expect, but she's just the nicest, most down-to-earth person. Makes you forget how famous she is."

"Yeah," Jack muttered.

"Oh, and she told us the funniest story about a bar in Moscow that looked like a brothel," Mikey said, laughing. "And we texted Sara that she's friends with Mick. Sara was speechless, maybe for the first time ever."

"She's a remarkable woman," John said. "Did you know that she held book talks all over the Middle East, and even had secret meetings with women in some very dangerous places?"

"Yeah, Dad. I know," Jack said, unable to peel his eyes off Tess. "I'm gonna go outside and rescue her."

Jack walked to the front door, put his coat on, and stepped onto the porch. He stood for a moment, just smiling at Tess and soaking in the joyfulness of the scene. She sat up, covered in snow, and smiled at him, waving her arm for him to come join the fun. As he walked toward them, she whispered something to the boys. The three of them rushed to make an armload of snowballs and sprinted toward Jack, pummeling him. They all burst into laughter. "Oh, you're in trouble now," Jack said.

***

After drying off and changing into fresh clothes, Tess trotted downstairs. "Okay, Mary," she said, "I'm ready. How can I help?"

Jack put his arm around her and said, "I want to take you for a drive."

"Honey, I promised your mother I'd help with the cooking."

"I just want to show you around the old neighborhood. You can help later."

"Jack, I…"

"It's fine, dear. Go with Jack. Julie and I can manage. Surely, she can cut some vegetables with my supervision," Mary said.

Julie playfully rolled her eyes.

Tess looked at Jack, uncertainty on her face.

"You heard her, it's fine," Jack said.

"Yeah, okay," Tess muttered. She turned to Mary and said, "You can put me to work as soon as we're back."

Mary smiled.

"Come on, my love," Jack said, taking her hand. They grabbed their coats and headed out.

After slowly driving around the slushy streets for over an hour, Tess said, "Jack, what are we doing? I know you and I can't imagine it was important to you to show me your old school and a skating rink."

"I wanted to get you out of the house," he replied.

"But I promised your mother I'd help her. The whole point of being here is to spend time with your family, but instead, you're driving around looking at a post office."

"I thought you could use a break," he said. "I know how they can be."

"They're lovely. Is it me? Did I do something wrong?"

"Hang on," he said, looking for a place to pull over. Once the car was stopped, he turned to her, put his hand on her cheek, and said, "I just wanted to be alone with you." He leaned over and started kissing her, working his way from her mouth, to her neck, to her ear.

"Jack," she whispered, pulling away. "Did we really leave your family on Christmas Eve to make out in a rental car? I don't understand. Please, let's go back."

"Fine," he said, shifting into drive.

***

Tess and Mary were making the final preparations for dinner when Jack strolled into the kitchen.

"Do you guys need any help?" he asked.

"Now that Tess has taken over for Julie, I think we have it under control," Mary said.

Tess stopped mashing the potatoes and said, "Honey, your brother and his family are hanging out upstairs. Your dad's alone in the other room. Why don't you go sit with him?"

"Yeah, okay," Jack said. He walked into the living room, a bit dejected, and plopped down on the couch. "Hey, Dad."

John put his book down. "Smells good. Do they need any help in there?"

"They kicked me out. What are you reading?"

"World War II book. It's dense, but well-written. A lot of good men sacrificed everything for the freedoms we enjoy. The world would look a whole lot different without them. There's real honor in serving something greater than yourself, in serving your country."

"I know, Dad. I feel that way too."

"There's a big difference between being out there in the thick of it and, well..."

"What I did. Is that what you were going to say? That my work wasn't honorable?"

"No, Jack. I wasn't going to say that. I respect your military service and your work at the Bureau."

"But you don't respect me, is that it?"

"I don't respect how you treated this family. It's disgraceful. A man with real honor never forgets what matters most: family, community, country. Those are the values I tried to instill in you kids. You forgot all about family. Now you come here with your wife, a woman we've never met, and..."

"And what, she's not good enough for you either?" he said loudly.

"Tess is a fine woman, but she's..."

"Too good for me, right?" Before John could respond, Jack leapt up. "I don't know why I bother. You made up your mind about me a long time ago." He stormed out of the room.

***

After John recited a blessing for Christmas Eve dinner, Tess turned to Mary and said, "The table is beautiful." The snow had begun to fall again, and Mary was concerned they wouldn't be able to make it to church. Mikey and Jack assured her it would be fine. Trying to focus on something else, Mary asked Tess how she became a writer.

"I've loved writing since I was a little girl. I wrote short stories throughout my childhood. I wasn't very good at talking about my feelings, and I suppose writing gave me a place to put them. Soon, I found that I was writing about other people's feelings too. I started working on my first novel when I was about seventeen, and I finished it during college. I was lucky that I was able to publish it. Readers were gracious, so I was able to turn writing into a career. It's such a blessing to do something you truly love. I'm sure I would write even if it weren't my job; it's how I try to make sense of the world and my place in it."

Mary smiled.

Tess turned to Julie and asked, "Did you always want to be a nurse?"

Julie nodded. "I guess I wanted to help people. Mikey did too."

"That seems to run in this family," Tess said with a smile. "It's nice that you both do something you enjoy."

"Working in healthcare certainly has its ups and downs. Sometimes we work crazy hours, and what we do isn't always valued. It's tough with two kids," Julie said.

"Actually, we have an opportunity to buy into a medical supplies business, which would make things easier, but you need at least fifteen thousand dollars to get in, and we just haven't been able to scrape it together," Mikey said. "Tess, this might not be the right time, but we wanted to ask you about it, if you might be willing to..."

Jack dropped his fork on his plate, making a loud clanking sound. "You are *not* asking her for money!"

"Well, we were thinking it could be a loan, just to help us buy in," Mikey said.

"Sure, Jack and I are happy to give you the money. It doesn't have to be a loan," Tess said.

Jack turned to Tess. "You are not giving them your money."

"It's *our* money, Jack," Tess said softly.

"It's yours," he replied.

"What? We're not married anymore?" she asked, crinkling her nose. She turned back to Mikey and Julie. "Of course we'll give it to you. That sounds exciting. Tell me, what kind of supplies?"

Jack made a fist and banged the table so forcefully that all the dishes and silverware flew up in the air, creating a cacophony of noise when they landed. "Tess, I said no!" he bellowed.

Tess gasped. Everyone sat in stunned silence. After a moment passed, Tess lifted her face to look at the group. "I'm so sorry, Mary. Please excuse me. I need some air," she said, getting up and walking toward the front door.

Jack jumped up. "Tess," he hollered.

She turned to face him. "Do you remember when we got married, how happy I was to take your name? I don't know what's happened to that man. The only thing I know is that you obviously don't want me anywhere near your family, so I'm leaving."

"Tess," he called.

"Do not follow me," she said. She grabbed her coat and left, closing the front door gently behind her.

"Jack," Mary said softly.

He stood frozen, his arms at his side, his shoulders slumped.

"Jack, I don't know what's going on with you, but you need to go after your wife," John said.

"You heard what she said. She doesn't want me anywhere near her."

"Jack, you need to go after Tess right now," Mary said.

Before he could move, they heard a loud scream, the screech of tires, and more screaming. Jack flew out of the house with Mikey close behind. They saw a car in the middle of the street, and Tess lying motionless in front of it. "Oh my God! Oh my God!" Jack screamed, racing toward her.

Tess was lying unconscious on the ground, her eyes shut, snow falling on her serene face. The driver of the car was hysterical. "I'm so sorry. I'm so sorry. She just ran out into the street," he said, shaking.

A man was standing nearby with a little girl. "My daughter, my daughter was in the street. She was about to get hit. That woman ran up and shoved her out of the way."

"Someone call 911!" Jack screamed, as neighbors began coming outside.

"My wife is calling," the man said.

Jack and Mikey sat on the cold asphalt next to Tess. "Don't move her," Mikey instructed. He bent down, listening for her breath. "She's breathing." He pressed two fingers against her neck. "Her pulse is strong."

"What have I done?" Jack cried.

"Tess, can you hear us? Can you hear us?" Mikey asked.

After several long seconds, Tess opened her eyes.

"Baby, it's me, it's Jack."

"Jack," she wheezed.

"Don't talk. Don't say anything, sweetheart. You'll be okay," he said, stroking her hair, tears cascading down his face.

"Tess, don't move your head, but can you follow my finger with just your eyes?" Mikey asked, holding up a finger and moving it across her field of vision.

She followed his finger with her eyes. "Jack," she gasped.

"Don't say anything. Don't say anything, sweetheart."

She started to close her eyes.

"Open your eyes, Tess," Mikey said. "I need you to stay with us."

"Stay with us, baby. Just look at me," Jack said.

"I'm cold," she whispered.

"We need a coat!" Jack yelled.

The driver took off his coat and gave it to Jack, his hand trembling.

Jack lay the coat over Tess and lightly brushed the snow off her face. "It's okay baby, just keep your eyes open. I'm here. It's okay."

She started to close her eyes again.

"Tess, keep your eyes open," Mikey said.

"Stay with us, baby," Jack pleaded.

Soon, they heard sirens approaching. An ambulance, police car, and fire truck pulled up. The EMTs ordered Jack and Mikey to move out of the way. Jack stood helplessly to the side, working to choke back his tears. They stabilized Tess's back and head, lifted her onto a gurney, and loaded her into the ambulance.

"I'm riding with them," Jack said, hopping into the back.

"We'll meet you at the hospital," Mikey hollered.

The doors closed and the ambulance sped away into the night.

CHAPTER 7

Jack was slumped against the waiting room wall, gripping his head in his hands, when Mikey, Mary, and John rushed in.

"How's Tess?" Mikey asked, trying to catch his breath.

Jack cleared his throat. "I... I don't know. She was conscious, but they won't know anything until the scans come back."

"I brought your coat," Mary said, draping it on a chair.

Jack broke down into hysterical tears.

"Oh honey," Mary said, resting her hand on his shoulder.

"It's my fault. This is all my fault," he sobbed, his mouth quivering.

She put her arms around him and held him as he wailed, his body heaving.

"It was an accident," Mary said softly.

"I drove her out of the house. I promised to take care of her. I promised to always protect her," he wheezed. "This is my responsibility."

"Thinking that way isn't going to help anyone, certainly not Tess. You're doing everything you can," Mary said.

Jack straightened up and wiped his face. In between sobs, he said, "I love her so much. She's everything to me. Everything. She was just trying to be nice, like she always is, and I... I did this."

Mary looked sternly at John, silently prodding him to offer some words of support.

"I can't believe this happened," John mumbled.

"I did this. I did this," Jack muttered.

John took a deep breath and said, "There's enough blame to go around." He walked over to Jack and placed a hand on his shoulder. "I should have made things easier for you. It's my fault you were so wound up. I'm sorry. And your mother's right: what Tess needs right now is our prayers and for you to have a level head. Take a seat, please. We're all here together."

"Yeah, okay," he sniffled, sitting down.

Mary sat beside him, rubbing his back.

"Jack, Tess is a wonderful woman," John said. "Your mother and I are very happy that you have her."

"She's amazing," Mikey said. "We all think so."

Jack sighed heavily, barely holding himself together.

"We've all fallen in love with her," Mary said.

"She's easy to love," Jack said.

"She has such a spirit of kindness and joy about her," Mary said.

"I'm not surprised by what she did tonight. She's always selfless. On the night that I proposed, we had left a bar with some of our friends, and there was a homeless man outside, Henry. I know his name because Tess stopped to introduce herself; she gave him money and held his hands. Then, as if that weren't enough, she took the scarf off her neck and handed it to him, insisting he take it because it was getting cold out." He stopped to compose himself. "Dad, I know you think I'm not good enough for her, but I've always known that. I've known it since the night we met. She could have been with anyone. You have no idea how lucky I've felt that she somehow chose me," he whimpered.

"We don't think that, Jack," John said.

"Honey, do you know what Tess told me over coffee this morning? She said, 'Jack is a little nervous, so you may not be seeing him at his best, but you raised an incredible man. He's kind and generous and a wonderful husband. I love him more than I could possibly tell you.' And I can see that, Jack. I see the way you look at each other. It's obvious how much she loves you and how much you love her," Mary said.

"Thanks," he muttered.

"We're all praying for her. That's what we can do right now. I believe in my heart that she will be all right. Is there anyone I should call?" Mary asked.

"Omar, Tess's best friend. He's her family every bit as much as I am. I have to call him. Before we got married, he made me promise to take care of her. I don't know how I'm going to tell him this. It was my fault," he said, breaking down into tears again.

"Jack, it was an accident," Mary said, handing him a tissue.

Jack wiped his face and excused himself to make the call. He returned a few minutes later, taking the seat next to his mother.

Every time a nurse or doctor walked by, he looked up anxiously. Soon, two police officers arrived, asking to question Tess. The nurse informed them that they would have to wait. They headed to the vending machine for coffee. A few minutes later, a local news crew showed up. "We heard Tess Lee saved a child's life tonight," the reporter said.

Jack sprang up and got in his face. "Get out of here," he bellowed.

"A world-famous author's act of heroism on Christmas Eve is quite a story," the reporter replied smugly. "I'm just the first one here. There will be others."

"You will *not* exploit this. Get out of here or I'll fucking kill you," Jack seethed. "Then you'll have a goddamn story."

Mikey jumped up and put his hand on Jack's arm. "The last thing Tess needs is for you to get arrested. You won't be here when she needs you. Seriously, you need to calm down. I'll get rid of them."

Jack wrenched away from his brother and grumbled, "Fine." He sat back down next to Mary in a huff.

Mikey quietly asked the receptionist to order the media to wait outside. He came back and told Jack, "I know everyone who works here. Let me handle it. I can keep them away from her."

"Thank you."

"I'm so sorry about what happened at dinner. I didn't mean…" Mikey said.

Jack cut him off. "It was my fault."

The minutes ticked by slowly. Eventually, a doctor emerged. "Mr. Miller?"

Jack jumped up. "How's my wife?"

"She's remarkably lucky. She suffered no internal injuries."

Jack inhaled deeply, relief sweeping across his face.

"Oh honey, thank God," Mary said, hugging him.

The doctor continued, "She has a mild concussion, a pretty nasty scrape on her arm, which is being bandaged, and some major bruising on her left arm, torso, and leg. The bruises will be worse tomorrow. We want to observe her for another two hours, but then you can take her home. She's refusing any prescription pain meds, so we need you to see that she takes ibuprofen regularly. A nurse will give you a bottle, along with further instructions and warnings signs that would require you to bring her back to the hospital. You need to see that she takes it easy. No physical activity for at least forty-eight hours. She shouldn't overexert herself. She should also avoid stress. I know you're from out of town, but I'd prefer if she didn't travel for at least five days. I can't imagine she'd feel up to it anyway. The bruising is significant and will take several weeks to heal, during which she should rest and stay off her feet as much as possible."

"I understand," Jack said.

"Mr. Miller, your wife has an unusually high tolerance for pain. It's quite remarkable. I suspect that what she reports as a level five pain would be an eight or nine for most people. If she reports a high level of pain, you should know it's actually sky-high."

"Can I see her?" Jack asked.

"Yes, she's been asking for you. The police want to question her first; they said it will only take a few minutes. When they're done, a nurse will come get you."

"Thank you, doctor. Thank you for everything," Jack said.

The doctor shook his head. "Truthfully, I think it's a Christmas miracle."

***

Ten minutes later, Jack saw the police officers leaving. He approached them and asked, "What did my wife say?"

"She corroborated exactly what the witnesses reported. The little girl darted into the middle of the street, and Mrs. Miller ran and pushed her out of the way. With it happening so fast and the snow falling, there was no way the driver could have anticipated it. He slammed on his brakes as fast as he could, but she said that there was nothing else he could have done. She said he was driving slowly, definitely not speeding, which is consistent with the tire marks at the scene."

"Thanks," Jack said.

"Before she would answer a single question, she insisted on information about the little girl. She wanted to know if she was all right, and she asked what her name is."

Jack smiled.

"Your wife saved her life, no question. A kid that size, it would have been catastrophic. Your wife is a hero. We're glad she'll be okay."

"Yeah, me too," Jack muttered. He started to walk away, paused, then turned and called, "What's the girl's name?"

"Genevieve. She's four years old. She and her folks are visiting her grandparents for the holiday. She ran outside because she thought she saw Santa's sleigh. When her father noticed, he sprinted after her, but she was already in the street. He screamed and your wife saw what was happening, and you know the rest."

"Thank you," Jack said.

A nurse came over and said, "Mr. Miller, I can take you to see your wife now."

***

Jack stood outside Tess's room, inhaled deeply to steady himself, and stepped inside.

Tess was sitting in bed, propped up against pillows. "Hey," she said softly.

He burst into tears.

"Didn't they tell you? I'll be fine."

"Yeah," he said, wiping his eyes. He walked over, pulled a chair beside her bed, and took her hand. "Sweetheart, I'm so sorry. I'm so sorry."

"It was an accident. It's no one's fault."

"No, I'm sorry for everything."

"Jack, I know that it's been really hard for you to be here, but the way you've been acting, I don't understand. Please help me understand."

"I gave up on having my family in my life a long time ago. The nature of my job made it impossible. I was undercover for months on end, sometimes longer, and it was extremely dangerous. When I finally took a desk job, I thought about reaching out but I didn't feel like I had the right to. Soon after that, I found out about Gracie, and when she died, I just didn't think I could ever face my parents. I had accepted it. Then I met you." He stopped to stroke her cheek. "You became my family, Tess."

"You don't have to choose. You deserve everything good in this life, Jack. I like your family a lot. I'm happy to spend time with them. Do you have any idea how lucky you are to have them? I would have given anything to be a part of a family like yours."

"You are a part of my family," he said.

"The whole time we've been here, it's like you don't want them to like me, like you're trying to create distance between us, like you're trying to sabotage the trip."

"They do like you. In fact, they're completely in love with you," he said.

"I don't understand the way you've been behaving," she said. "Something changed as soon as we got here."

"Tess, these past three years with you have been the happiest of my life. I don't have the words to tell you how much you mean to me. When we got here, I panicked and became horribly insecure. My father doesn't think much of me, never has, and they were all so caught up in you being Tess Lee. I didn't want them to make you uncomfortable and ruin the only good thing I've ever had. I was trying to protect you and us, even though I know I went about it all wrong. I was worried that they would say or do something to make you love me less."

"Honey, no one could ever make me love you less, although you've been giving it a pretty good go."

He laughed. He took her hand in both of his, caressing her skin. "Tess, please forgive me. I promise to spend every day of the rest of my life making it up to you."

"Jack, there's nothing to forgive. But I do want you to do something for me."

"Anything."

"When we get back to your parents' house, you need to sit them down and tell them about your job. You need to explain why you were out of touch for so many years. You should find a time to tell Mikey too; he looks up to you and it hurt him more than he'll admit. It's clear they have no idea the sacrifices you've made. I'll be by your side, holding your hand the whole time. They're good people, and they'll understand. Will you please do this for me?"

"Yes."

"Good. Now take off your shoes and climb into bed," she said. "I want to feel your arms."

He took his shoes off. She scooched over, wincing when she moved.

"Oh sweetheart, are you in a lot of pain?"

She shook her head. "I'm just a little sore. I'll feel better with you here. Just don't touch me over there," she said, pointing to her left side.

"The doctor said you have an unusually high tolerance for pain."

"They don't call me the high priestess of pain for nothing," she said, smiling.

He climbed into bed and lay facing her, carefully putting one arm around her, and his other hand on her cheek. He pressed his lips gently to hers. "Tess, I love you with my whole heart, forever," he whispered, and he kissed her again.

She rested her forehead against his and closed her eyes. "When we were in the bar last night and then at dinner tonight, I thought maybe you wished you hadn't married me. But I knew you'd come back to me."

"Sweetheart, I never left. My problem is that I love you so much sometimes I can't see straight."

"I love you too, more than anything," she said.

"You know you saved that little girl's life."

"Anyone would have done the same thing."

"It's so like you to say that," he said.

"She's only four years old, the same age Gracie was."

"Yeah, I know," he whispered, and he kissed her forehead. "The media's here, waiting outside the hospital. Everyone's calling you a hero."

"Jack, I don't want..."

"Don't worry. Mikey is taking care of it. You won't have to see them."

"Thank you."

"He's in the waiting room with my folks. They've been so worried about you. My mother's been praying nonstop. Julie's been texting for updates every five minutes; she had to stay at the house with the boys."

"They're here? But your mother was looking forward to going to church. Oh, I feel terrible."

"Don't be silly," he said, rubbing her head. "Of course they're here. They're our family."

She smiled.

"That reminds me, we should probably call Omar. I texted him when we got word you were okay, but I know he wants to hear from you."

"I wish you wouldn't have worried him."

"Are you kidding? I had to call him. He and I have an understanding about you that I can't break. He's your family. He wanted to catch the first flight here, but I told him to wait."

"Let's FaceTime him so he can see I'm fine," Tess said.

Jack pulled out his phone and called Omar. He answered immediately. "There's someone here who wants to say hello," Jack said, and he positioned the phone so they were both in the frame.

"Butterfly, oh my God. Are you okay? I've been a nervous wreck. I can hop on the next flight. Things are a bit backed up with the holiday and the snow, but I can be there in..."

Tess chuckled and interrupted him. "No need. I'm fine, really. Just a few scrapes and bruises. It's nothing. We were in worse shape after that nightclub in Mykonos."

Omar laughed. "I know you're going for some kind of sainthood, Butterfly, but bloody hell, saving a small child on Christmas Eve – isn't that a bit much?"

She giggled.

"I know you're with Jack, but I really am happy to come. Are you sure you don't want me there?"

"Jack's taking good care of me, I promise. In a few days, you can see for yourself. I'm fine. I might even have a couple of cool scars to lend me some distinction."

"That's the spirit," Omar said. "I love you. I love you beyond measure. Clay sends his love too."

"I love you both. Bye."

Jack put his phone away. Just then, a nurse walked in. "Uh, this is not allowed. I'm sorry, but you'll need to get out of that bed, Mr. Miller."

"I'm not moving," he replied.

"It really is making me feel better. Please let him stay," Tess said.

The nurse smiled. "Well, it is Christmas Eve and you are everyone's favorite patient, plus you saved a child's life. I suppose I can look the other way. But he needs to be seated in that visitor's chair when the doctor comes in for his final check."

"I promise he will be. Thank you, Regina," Tess said.

"I'll be back to check on you in half an hour. Then the doctor will see you and spring you from this place. Use the call button if you need me." Regina offered a small wink and then left the pair alone.

Jack stroked Tess's hair, looking into her eyes.

"Tell me you love me," she whispered.

"I love you, Tess Miller. I love you with my whole heart, forever."

She smiled.

"Now you tell me something," he said.

"What?"

"I want to hear about that nightclub in Mykonos."

She giggled and rolled her eyes dramatically.

***

After the doctor signed off on Tess's release, a nurse came to give Jack instructions, including dangerous concussion signs to watch for and how to change the bandage on her arm. "She really needs to take it easy. She'll be in a lot of discomfort, so she'll require help getting dressed and undressed, sitting and standing, you get the picture." She handed him two bottles of pills. "We're sending her home with a high dosage ibuprofen and something stronger, in case she changes her mind."

"Thank you," Jack said.

"The media has swarmed the front entrance, but I think your family has come up with a plan to get her out of here. Why don't you go talk with them and I'll help her use the bathroom and get dressed?"

"Okay," he said. He bent down and kissed Tess's head. "I'll be right back, sweetheart."

He joined his family in the waiting room. They all leapt to their feet, eager for news. "How's she doing?" Mary asked.

"She's all right. I can tell she's in pain, but Tess never complains."

"We'll take good care of her," John said.

"Of course, anything she needs. You two can stay as long as you like. We want to help," Mary said.

"She felt badly that you missed church because of her."

Mary smiled. "How silly. That's not important. She's such a sweet girl."

"Yeah," Jack muttered. "Thank you all for staying."

"We're family. There's nowhere else we would be," John said.

"Tess is very private. We have to keep the media away from her," Jack said.

"We're all over it," Mikey said. "We brought two cars. We're going to leave out the front entrance. Mom and Dad will head home, and will make a bit of a fuss on the way out to distract the reporters. Meanwhile, I'll pull my rental car around to the delivery entrance. One of the nurses will bring you and Tess there."

"Thank you," Jack said. He hugged his mother and headed back to retrieve Tess. When he got to her room, she was sitting in a wheelchair, dressed and ready to go.

"This is ridiculous," she protested. "I can walk."

"Everyone gets wheeled out, it's standard protocol," the nurse said. "And you *were* hit by a car a few hours ago. That's pretty major. You really need to take it easy and stay off your feet for at least a few weeks. Your body has been through something traumatic. It will take time."

"Fine. Thank you, Regina," she said.

Jack walked beside them as the nurse wheeled Tess down the corridor to a freight elevator, and all the way to the delivery entrance. On the way, Tess thanked each doctor, nurse, and orderly by name. Mikey was waiting for them by the loading dock. As Jack helped Tess up, she turned to Regina and said, "Thank you for taking such good care of me."

"You really are everyone's favorite patient. I didn't want to tell you this before, but I'm such a huge fan. I read your books on my breaks, especially on hard days. They lift my spirits. They mean a lot to me. Thank you."

"You're very kind," Tess replied.

Jack helped her into the backseat and sat right beside her. She rested her head on his shoulder and they drove off.

***

When they got to the house, John, Mary, and Julie were waiting for them.

"Oh Tess, thank God you're okay. I've been praying for you all night. We're going to take good care of you. Don't worry about a thing. Come sit down, honey," Mary said, guiding her to the couch.

Jack helped her sit down and everyone continued to fuss.

"We've been so worried. The boys made you these," Julie said, handing her two welcome home cards made from construction paper and marker.

Tess grinned. "That's so sweet."

"They wanted to wait up for you, but we thought you'd prefer the quiet," Julie said.

Jack turned to Mikey. "Yeah, actually, we were hoping to speak to Mom and Dad alone, if you don't mind."

"Of course not," Mikey said. He looked at Tess, "I'm so glad you're okay. Please wake me if you need anything at all." He turned to Jack, "Seriously, wake me if anything changes."

Jack nodded.

"Thank you for everything," Tess said.

"Yeah, thank you," Jack said, outstretching his hand.

"No way, man," Mikey said, throwing his arms around him in a bear hug.

Everyone smiled and Mikey and Julie headed upstairs.

Mary came to sit beside Tess. She took her hands and started to cry. "Tess, we've been friends with Rosalie and Frank Patterson for over thirty years. Genevieve is their granddaughter." She paused, trying to catch her breath. "You saved her life tonight. You're such a brave girl. We can never thank you enough."

"There's no need to thank me. I just did what anyone would have done. I'm so glad Genevieve wasn't hurt."

"You're a hero," John said. "What you did for that family isn't something anyone around here will forget."

"Really, anyone would have done the same," Tess said.

"You're a dear, dear girl. We're so glad you're a part of this family," Mary said, squeezing Tess's hands. She stood up, pulled a tissue out of her pocket, and blew her nose. "I need to clean my face. Tess, are you hungry? I can get you something to eat."

"Thank you, but I'm fine," she replied.

"How about a cup of herbal tea?" Mary asked.

"That would be perfect. Thank you."

Jack took Mary's place on the sofa beside Tess. He wrapped an arm around her shoulder. "How are you doing, sweetheart?"

She smiled and nuzzled into him. "Better with you here."

Soon, Mary returned carrying a tray with four teacups. John stood to help her pass out the steaming tea, and then she and John sat down in their reclining chairs.

"We wanted to talk with you both," Tess said. "I don't think Jack has ever told you the nature of the work he did and why he was out of touch for so long. I think it's something you should hear." She interlaced her fingers with Jack's and said, "Go on, honey. Tell them."

Jack took a deep breath and began. "I didn't have a desk job until the end of my time with the FBI. For most of my career, I was a field agent doing counterterrorism work, mostly deep undercover, very dangerous stuff." Mary and John's mouths fell open. Jack continued, proceeding to tell them everything about his time in the field, only leaving out the violence they didn't need to know about.

At one point, Tess interjected. "He earned a Medal of Valor, and later an FBI Shield of Bravery for his work bringing down a terrorist cell. He put his own life on the line and saved countless innocent people."

Jack looked at her, surprised.

"Joe told me two years ago. He assumed I knew," she whispered. She turned back to Mary and John. "He's very humble."

Mary had been weeping silently as Jack spoke. "Honey, we had no idea."

Jack looked down, a hint of shame on his face.

"He does care about family, more than anything. He's been protecting American families for his entire life at great personal sacrifice and without any thought for himself. He's an extraordinary man," Tess said.

John started to cry. He regained his composure and said, "Jack, I don't know what to say. We were devastated when you cut us off. Why didn't you ever tell us?"

"I was trying to protect you. I never wanted to put you in harm's way. Field agents don't get to have families. Plus, I remember how worried Mom was each time you were called to a fire. I didn't want to put her through that again, especially when I was completely off the grid for months at a time. I thought I was making it easier for you both. I'm sorry," Jack said.

John wiped the corners of his eyes and stood up. Jack rose and John scooped him into a tight hug. "We're very proud of you, son."

"Thanks, Dad," Jack said, through tears.

After they finally sat down, Jack grabbed Tess's hand, lifted it to his lips, and kissed it gently.

"Tess, we know this is your doing. It's been unbearable without Jack, without knowing what we could have done differently. I don't know what to say or how we could ever thank you for making our family whole again," John said.

Tess smiled. "There's no need. I just thought you should know who your son is."

"You know the best thing Jack has ever done?" Mary said. "He gave us you."

"I couldn't agree more," Jack said.

Tess blushed. "You're all very sweet."

Jack kissed her temple. "I think I should get Tess to bed. She's supposed to rest." He helped Tess up, noticing her wince when she moved. "Come on, sweetheart. Let's get some sleep; it's after midnight."

"It's Christmas," Mary said.

"Merry Christmas," Tess said.

"Merry Christmas, you darling girl," Mary replied.

***

"Sweetheart, tell me what you need and I'll get it," Jack said.

"My gray pajamas. They're in the top drawer." He got the pajamas and handed them to her. "Thanks. I'm going to wash my face and brush my teeth."

"Call me if you need anything. I'll help you get dressed."

Ten minutes later, Tess was still in the bathroom and Jack heard squealing noises like she was in pain. "Sweetheart, are you all right?" he called.

"I'm okay," she said in a distressed voice.

When she emerged, she was wearing her pajamas. "I left my clothes on the floor and had trouble bending over to get them."

"Baby, why didn't you let me help you get dressed?"

"I didn't want you to see," she said quietly.

"Tess, I don't care…"

She shook her head. "I don't mean it like that. It's not vanity. I just didn't want to upset you."

"Is it that bad?" he asked.

She nodded faintly.

"Sweetheart, I can handle it. Please, let me take care of you."

"Okay," she whispered.

He kissed her tenderly. "Here," he said, handing her two pills and a glass of water. "It's time for your meds." She swallowed the pills and placed the water on her nightstand.

"I'm so tired," she said.

"Come on, let's get you in bed." He pulled the comforter down and helped her into bed. She flinched several times. Once she was lying down, he said, "I'll be right back." He darted into the bathroom and came out a few minutes later wearing sweatpants and a T-shirt. He climbed into bed beside her and switched off the light. He lay on his side, touching her face. "I love you so much; I don't even have words for it."

"I love you more than anything," she replied. "Jack, I never told you what happened, with the accident."

"The police told me."

"But I never told you," she said.

"What is it?" he asked, stroking her hair.

"The whole thing happened in an instant. I heard a man scream and I looked and saw this little girl, headlights coming at her. When I got to her, there was only time to shove her out of the way, it happened so fast. All I could think is that you would be left thinking I had been mad at you. That's what I was trying to tell you in the street and in the ambulance, but you kept telling me not to talk. Jack, I couldn't bear it if something happened to either of us and we were like that."

"It was my fault," he said.

"No, honey. My point is that we can never forget, not even for a moment, to just love each other. Nothing else matters."

He kissed her softly. "I promise. I love you so much."

She traced his jawline with her finger. "I'm glad your parents have a chance to see the kind of man you really are, and why I'm so madly in love with you."

"I don't know how to thank you for helping me have that conversation. It never would have happened without you."

"I'll keep saying this until you believe it: you deserve every happiness in this life, Jack. I know you struggle with the things you've had to do, with the darkness, and so you don't always know that, but I do."

He smiled.

"I want you to do something tomorrow," she said.

"Anything."

"Give Mikey and Julie the money they asked for. Actually, you should give them more than what they asked for, and you have to make him see that it's a gift, not a loan."

"Tess…"

"Please, just listen to me. It's like at the bar the other night when I didn't have money for the jukebox, and Mikey gave me three dollars."

"They're not asking for three dollars."

"It doesn't matter. What they're asking for means less to us than those three dollars did to him, and he gave it to me without a moment's hesitation. When you have something someone needs, you give it to them. If I had a loving family, don't you think the first thing I would have done when I had the means would have been to take care of them? That's what people do. That's why I paid for Omar's education. You should do whatever you think is right to financially help your parents and siblings. We have more money than we could spend in several lifetimes. They're your family. Please, Jack."

"Okay."

"Kiss me," she said.

He pressed his lips to hers. "You always think of everyone else, even when you're hurt. What do *you* want?" he asked.

"You. The only thing I want is you."

"You've got me, sweetheart. You've got me."

CHAPTER 8

When Tess woke up the next morning, Jack's hand was on her stomach. She touched his fingers.

"Hey, sweetheart," he whispered.

"What time is it?" she asked.

He craned his neck to look at the clock. "Almost eight. You need to take your pills. How do you feel?"

"I've been better." She sat up slowly, wincing and making several pained noises.

"Here, take these," he said.

She swallowed the pills. "Thank you."

"You should stay in bed and rest. I can bring you anything you need."

"It's Christmas. We should spend the day with your family."

"Sweetheart, everyone will understand."

"Please Jack. I'm not staying in bed all day. I want to see everyone."

"Omar warned me you'd refuse to take it easy."

"There's no difference if I sit in bed or sit on the couch. I want to get up."

"Only if you promise to tell me the truth about how you feel and let me help you."

She nodded.

He got out of bed and took her hand, guiding her to her feet. "How bad is it?" he asked.

"A seven."

He kissed the top of her head.

"I'm going to use the bathroom and brush my teeth," she said.

"Sweetheart, I can help you with the toilet. They said sitting and standing would be difficult."

"I'll manage. You can help with everything else." She shuffled to the bathroom. Jack heard several groans and a soft, muffled scream. She returned a few minutes later. "I need to take a shower and get dressed, but I don't think I can do it by myself."

"That's what I'm here for," he said. "I'll get your clothes and put them on the bed. You could just wear pajamas if it's more comfortable."

"It's Christmas. There's no way I'm wearing pajamas."

"Tess, you were hit by a car fifteen hours ago. No one will care."

"You said you'd help me. Please, Jack."

"Okay, baby. Tell me what to get."

"In the closet, I have black pants and a black silk top. It's the most comfortable outfit I brought. I'll need a black bra and underwear too."

He retrieved the items and carefully placed them on the bed.

"I'll need shoes too," she said.

"Tess…"

"I'll need shoes," she repeated firmly.

"Which pair?"

"The patent leather ones."

He got the shoes and put them on the floor by the bed. "I'll help you shower, change your bandage, and get you dressed. All you have to do is tell me if something hurts too much, okay?"

She nodded. "Thank you."

He took Tess's hand and led her to the bathroom. He turned the shower on and faced her. "Are you able to lift your arms?" She raised her arms, wincing the whole time, and he gently pulled her top over her head. He crouched down and gingerly pulled her pajama pants down. She put her hands on his shoulders and stepped out of one leg at a time. He gently pulled her underwear down and she slowly stepped out of those as well. When he saw the massive dark purple and red bruising along her body, he whispered, "Oh sweetheart. I'm so sorry. I had no idea."

"It looks worse than it is," she said softly.

He stood and kissed the top of her head. "I need to take your bandage off."

She outstretched her arm and he carefully removed the bandage, revealing a nasty scrape. They looked into each other's eyes and he brushed the side of her face before taking off his clothes. "Do you want me to put your hair up?" he asked.

She nodded. He grabbed a scrunchie and pulled her hair into a loose bun at the nape of her neck. "I'll step in first," he said, getting into the shower. He reached for her hand and she slowly stepped in. When the water hit her body, she started to tremble. He cradled her face in his hands. "I've got you. Just look into my eyes." Their eyes locked, and soon she stopped shaking. He lathered a washcloth with soap and gently washed her entire body. When she flinched, he looked into her eyes and she stared into his. After rinsing off, he turned the faucet off, climbed out, and guided her behind him. He threw a towel around his waist and then took a fresh towel and gently patted her body dry, from her shoulders down to her toes. Kneeling on the floor, he held her underwear and she stepped into them, one foot at a time. He gently pulled them up and then took a dry towel and wrapped it around her. He put the toilet seat down. "Sit here," he said, helping her. She let her hair down and got the bandaging supplies ready. She extended her arm and he gently dressed her wound. "Does that feel okay?" he asked. She nodded. He quickly dried himself off and threw on sweatpants. "Let's get you dressed," he said.

They walked into the bedroom and he put her bra on, slipped her shirt over her head, and crouched on the floor so she could step into her pants. He carefully pulled them up and zipped them. He knelt again and held out one shoe at a time. Balancing on his shoulders, she stepped into each one. When he stood up, he whispered, "Just one more thing." He retrieved her heart locket from the dresser. She smiled and held her hair aside while he fastened the chain. "There," he said. "You're perfect."

Her eyes became watery. "Oh sweetheart, are you in terrible pain?" he asked, gently wiping away her tears.

She shook her head. "It's just the opposite. I didn't think it was possible to love you more."

"We're as close as two people can be. We always will be." He kissed her forehead and helped her sit in the chair in the corner of the room. "Just wait here. I'll shave and throw on my clothes as quickly as I can."

"Jack," she called. He turned to face her. She just stared at him, and he stared back, each with a soft smile, no words spoken.

***

They walked downstairs, hand in hand.

Everyone was sitting quietly in the living room. They all jumped up when they noticed Tess and Jack. "Oh, you're awake," Mary said, rushing over. "How are you feeling?"

"I'm okay," Tess said. "Merry Christmas!"

"Merry Christmas," everyone said, less than enthusiastically.

Jack could see that they all looked distressed. "Mikey, what's going on?"

"The media is camped out on the lawn, local and national. There's a whole army of them."

"What?" Tess asked.

"This is the last thing Tess needs. She's supposed to avoid stress," Jack said.

"We closed all the blinds, but we didn't know what else to do," Mary said.

Tess walked over to a window and peeked through the blinds. "Oh my God," she mumbled. She turned to everyone, hot tears streaming down her face. "I'm so sorry. I've ruined your Christmas."

"Don't be silly," Mary said. "Please don't be upset, dear. You need to focus on getting well. That's the only thing that matters. We couldn't care less. We were just concerned it would bother you."

Tess looked at Jack. He put his arm around her. "I'll get rid of these assholes."

"Jack, please. I know you mean well, but you're angry and only going to make it worse," Tess said.

John interjected, "Son, I would like to go outside. I think I can say something to get rid of them, but I didn't want to do anything without your permission. I'd like to try if you'll let me."

Jack looked at Tess. She wiped her face and nodded.

"Okay, Dad," Jack said.

"Trust me, I promise I won't violate your privacy, Tess. I'll even leave the door ajar. You can stand out of sight and listen," John said.

"Thank you."

John put on his coat and walked outside, leaving Tess standing behind the slightly open door.

The reporters rushed forward with their microphones and cameras, shouting a thousand questions.

John held up a hand to silence them and began speaking. "No one else from my family is going to come outside and speak with you. What I have to say is all that you'll get, and I won't be answering any questions. Last night, my daughter-in-law committed a truly selfless act. What she wants now is to recover and celebrate the holiday in private with her husband Jack and our family. I'm appealing to your sense of decency and asking you to honor her selflessness with your own act of selflessness. Please respect her wishes and leave." He stood stoically. One reporter signaled to her cameraman and he turned off his equipment. One by one, they put away their gear, nodded at John, and left. When the last person drove away, John went back inside. He locked the door and turned to Tess, who had tears in her eyes.

"It's okay. They're gone now," he said.

"Thank you," she said softly. She sniffled and wiped her eyes. "It's just… I never had a father who would do that for me."

"You do now," John said. "I would hug you, but I don't want to hurt you."

They both smiled and joined everyone in the living room.

"Thank you, Dad," Jack said.

John nodded.

"Now you need to get off your feet," Mary said to Tess. "Would you be more comfortable on the couch or in a chair?"

"On the couch with Jack, please," Tess said.

Jack walked her over to the sofa and helped her sit down before taking the seat beside her. He brushed his hand on her thigh and she rubbed her fingers against his.

"Mikey, would you please go get Tess and Jack some coffee? Tess takes it black," Mary said. She turned to Tess. "You must be starving, dear. We've kept everything warm in the kitchen. There are pancakes, French toast, scrambled eggs, fruit salad, and of course I can make you anything else you like."

"Scrambled eggs would be perfect. Thank you," Tess replied.

"I'll fix you a plate, Jack," Mary said.

"Mom, why don't you stay here and keep Tess company. I want to speak with Mikey," Jack said. He leaned over and asked Tess, "Will you be okay alone for a minute?"

"Of course. And I'm not alone; I'm with our family."

Jack pecked her cheek and went to the kitchen.

"Hey, I was just going to bring these to you guys," Mikey said, holding two mugs of coffee.

Jack took the mugs and put them down on the counter.

"How's Tess doing?" Mikey asked. "I figured she'd be up in bed for at least a few days, if not weeks."

"She's tough. She always puts on a brave face and she's not good at taking care of herself," Jack said.

"That's what she has you for," Mikey said.

"Yeah," Jack chuckled. He pulled a folded check out of his pocket and handed it to his brother.

Mikey opened it and his eyes went wide. It was made out for thirty thousand dollars. "Jack, I can't take this," he said, trying to return it. "Julie and I feel awful about what happened. I never should have asked you guys."

Jack shook his head. "It was me. It was my fault. Tess is the most generous person I've ever known. She was horrified by my behavior. She wouldn't have thought twice about giving it to you, and I shouldn't have either. Sometimes I'm just overprotective of her. You're my brother and I love you. Please accept it. We both want you to have it."

"We'll pay you back," Mikey said.

"Please don't. It's a gift. Please just take it and use it for your family."

"Thank you," Mikey said quietly.

"We're also setting up college funds for the boys and for Sara's little girl. Whatever aspirations your kids have for their futures, you won't have to worry about it. It'll be taken care of."

"Jack, I don't know what to say."

"Don't say anything. Tess and I are happy to do it. She's taught me a lot about how to treat people, especially the ones you care about. I know the burden I placed on you and Sara when I disappeared. Money can't change it, but I want to try to make it right."

Mikey smiled and extended his hand, but Jack threw his arms around him instead and they hugged.

"I really missed you," Mikey said. "I'm so glad you're back."

"Me too," Jack said. "I'm gonna grab some food. Do you mind bringing the coffee in?"

"You got it."

***

When Tess and Jack finished eating, Mary took their plates to the kitchen. When she returned, she announced, "It's time for presents! The boys have been very patient."

"You haven't opened presents yet?" Tess asked.

"Of course not, dear. We were waiting for you," Mary replied.

The boys tore into their Santa Claus presents first, red and green bits of wrapping paper flying around the room. Jack put his arm around Tess, and she burrowed into him. "How are you feeling?" he whispered.

"Sore, but I'm okay."

Soon they were all opening family presents. The boys went nuts for their new video games and excused themselves to go play. Julie loved her periwinkle cashmere scarf, immediately wrapping it around her neck. "It's beautiful. Thank you so much," she said.

"You're welcome. We got the same one for Sara in red," Tess replied.

"Oh, I can't wait to bake with this," Mary said, admiring her new stand mixer.

"This is the nicest fishing gear I've ever had," John said. "I can't believe you remembered our fishing excursions."

Jack smiled at Tess, kissing her cheek several times and squeezing her hand each time a new gift was opened.

Once the floor was covered in tattered paper and ribbons, Mary looked at Tess and Jack and said, "Don't you two have presents for each other?"

"We don't buy each other presents," Jack said.

"Each year at the holidays, we make a donation to our favorite charity instead. When Jack and I were dating, he gave me this necklace," Tess said, holding her locket. "I told him it was the best gift I'd ever received and that he was never to buy me another thing because nothing else would ever be as good."

Jack pulled Tess to him and kissed her forehead.

Mary smiled at them. "Well, Tess, we all got you a present." She retrieved a box from under the tree and handed it to Tess. It was beautifully wrapped in shiny, silver paper with a gold bow.

"You really didn't have to do this," Tess said.

As she began unwrapping the package, Mary said, "I'm sure you write your books on a computer, but we thought maybe you could use this for book signings or something, to remember that you're a part of our family."

Tess opened the box to find a sterling silver pen engraved with the name Tess Miller. Her eyes became misty. "Thank you," she said softly.

"I hope you like it, dear," Mary said.

"You've tied Jack for the best present I've ever received," she said, wiping her eyes.

***

Later that morning, they were all drinking coffee and talking when the doorbell rang.

"I'll get it," John said, rising from his recliner.

"Hi, Louise," he said, opening the door. "Merry Christmas."

Mary rushed over. "Merry Christmas, Louise," she said.

"Merry Christmas. I don't know if you've met my husband Todd and our daughter Genevieve," Louise said.

"Please come inside," Mary said, ushering them in.

Louise handed her a large cake dome. "My mother made you all a coffee cake. My folks wanted to come over, but we didn't want to overwhelm you. They're planning to stop by later if that's all right. We called the hospital several times last night and we heard that Tess was discharged. We were hoping to see her, if she's up to visitors."

"She's right here in the living room," Mary said, showing them the way. "Tess, this is Louise, our neighbor's daughter, and this is her husband Todd and their daughter Genevieve."

Tess started to rise but Louise stopped her. "Oh, please don't get up. We just wanted to come over to..." She burst into tears.

Todd rubbed her shoulders. "What she's trying to say is that we wanted to come over to thank you. We don't even know where to begin, don't have the words. What you did, well..."

"Please, you don't have to thank me. Anyone would have done the same thing."

Louise sniffled and said, "How are you feeling? Is there anything we can do for you?"

"Really, I'm just a little sore. I'll be fine, thank you," Tess replied. "How's Genevieve?"

"Well, she made you something and she has something she'd like to say to you," Louise said. She bent down in front of her daughter and said, "It's okay. You can go ahead."

Genevieve tentatively approached Tess and handed her a crayon drawing. "I made this for you."

"Thank you so much. It's beautiful. I'll put it up on my refrigerator when I get home, okay?"

Genevieve nodded. "Thank you for saving me."

"Oh, sweet girl, you're welcome."

"You pushed me," Genevieve said.

"I'm sorry I had to do that," Tess said. "It was all there was time for. Did you get a booboo?"

"Nope, but my mommy said you got a booboo."

"That's okay. It will feel better soon," Tess said.

"Can I hug it better?" Genevieve asked.

"I would love that," Tess said, and she leaned forward and opened her arms.

"Be gentle," Louise warned.

Genevieve collapsed into Tess's arms and they hugged for ages. When they parted, Tess said, "I need to ask you to do something for me. Please promise me that you'll never go into the street without holding a grown-up's hand."

"I promise," Genevieve said.

"That's a good girl. Now, if it's okay with your parents, we have Christmas cookies in the kitchen. Maybe you could pick a couple to take home for later."

Genevieve turned to her parents expectantly.

"Of course," Louise said.

"Jack, please help me up," Tess said. Jack stood up, took Tess's hand, and helped her slowly rise.

"Come on," she said to Genevieve, holding her hand. "Do you like chocolate chip or sprinkles?" Tess asked.

"Chocolate chip," Genevieve replied.

"That's what my husband Jack likes, too."

When they were out of the room, Todd turned to Jack. "I'm so sorry this happened to your wife. We feel terrible. I don't know how we'll ever be able to thank her. You can't imagine how scary it is to think that you're going to watch your child die."

"Actually, I can," Jack said. "I lost my little girl when she was around Genevieve's age."

"Oh Jack, we had no idea," Louise said. "We're so sorry."

"Thank you. You learn to live with it."

"Jack, I saw what happened last night," Todd said. "By the time I got outside, there was no way I could have gotten to her in time. I screamed and your wife didn't hesitate for a second, not a single second. She's very modest, but few would have done what she did. Most people would have hesitated or made the decision to stand on the sidelines. She was so selfless and brave. I'm a police officer up in Toledo, where we live. I've seen some courageous acts in my life, but nothing like what Tess did last night. The world should have more people like your wife."

Jack smiled.

Just then, Tess and Genevieve returned. Genevieve was holding a storage bag filled with cookies, and they were both wiping powdered sugar off their lips. Tess looked at Genevieve and they both giggled.

"You caught us; we shared a cookie," Tess said. She looked down at Genevieve and said, "Tell them why it's okay."

"Because we were in an accident, we get to have a cookie to feel better," Genevieve said.

Everyone smiled.

"We don't want to intrude, but please don't hesitate to let us know if there's anything we can do for you," Louise said to Tess. She reached out for her hands, squeezed them, and said, "Thank you. From the very bottom of my heart, thank you."

"You're welcome," Tess said, wiping her eyes.

"Merry Christmas, everyone," Louise said.

"Merry Christmas, Genevieve," Tess said.

"Merry Christmas, Tessie!" Genevieve said.

When they left, Jack put his arm around Tess. "How are you holding up, sweetheart?"

"I'm a little tired. I think I'd like to take a nap."

Jack walked Tess upstairs. He knelt on the floor and took her shoes off, one by one, and helped her into bed. "Please take these," he said, handing her ibuprofen. She swallowed the pills and rested her head on the pillow.

"I'm okay. You should go spend time with everyone," she said.

"I'll stay here until you fall asleep," he said, caressing her head. As soon as she fell asleep, he moved to the chair in the corner of the room, watching over her as she slept.

***

When Tess awoke, she stretched her arms and slowly sat up.

"Hey, you," Jack said.

"Have you been here this whole time?" she asked.

He nodded.

"What time is it?" she asked.

"A little after five."

"Oh Jack, you missed everything. Your mother has been cooking for days."

"I'm sure there's plenty left," he said, sitting on the edge of the bed. "How are you feeling?"

"The same. A little better maybe."

He picked up her hand and kissed it. "I can bring you something to eat."

She shook her head. "Let's go downstairs. Sara's probably here, and I'm eager to meet her. I just need to freshen up."

He helped her out of bed and into the bathroom. A few minutes later, he put her shoes on and they went downstairs.

Everyone was sitting in the living room, talking and nibbling on cheese and crackers.

"Jack!" Sara exclaimed, rushing over to hug him.

"Hey, rug rat," Jack said, squeezing her tightly.

She knuckled his arm. "I missed you so much."

"Me too," he said.

"This is my husband Bill."

They shook hands and Jack said, "This is Tess."

"It's lovely to meet you," Tess said.

"I've heard so much about you," Sara said. "From what I hear, we have two heroes in the house. Dad hasn't stopped bragging on you both."

Tess smiled and glanced at Jack. There was a lightness in his eyes she had never seen before.

"I would hug you, but I know you're injured," Sara said.

"That's okay," Tess said, hugging her gently.

Jack turned to his mother. "I'm sorry we missed Christmas dinner, Mom. I'm going to fix Tess something to eat."

"You didn't miss anything. We waited for you," Mary said. She turned to Tess. "If you're not feeling well enough, dear, I can bring you a plate upstairs."

"I'm okay. I'd prefer to sit with you all. You didn't have to wait."

"Nonsense," Mary replied. "I know you had plans to go home tomorrow, but John and I would very much like you to stay until you're recovered. We'll take good care of you. Please, will you and Jack stay?"

Tess nodded. "Thank you."

"The Pattersons stopped by to meet you and thank you for what you did for their granddaughter. They're going to come back tomorrow if you're up to company," Mary said.

Tess smiled.

"Everyone sit. Julie, Mikey, will you please come help me serve the food?" Mary asked.

Jack helped Tess sit at the dining room table and he took the chair beside her. Soon the table was overflowing with turkey and all the trimmings.

"Before we dig into this feast your mother prepared, I'd like to say a few words," John said. "Mary and I are elated to have all three of our children home this year. We are extremely proud of each of you. We're especially thankful that our oldest son has returned home. Julie and Bill, you already know how much we love you both. Tess, we love you too. We want you to know how grateful we are that you're a part of this family. We know that you weren't comfortable with the public attention over what happened last night, but privately, among our family, we'd like to acknowledge the sacrifice you made."

Everyone raised their glasses.

Tess blushed.

John continued. "We thank the Lord for this bounty and all the blessings bestowed upon this family. Amen."

Jack made Tess a plate with sweet potatoes, green beans, glazed carrots, and cranberry sauce. They all ate by the glow of the twinkling Christmas tree and the roar of the fireplace.

"Tess, I hear that a certain rock star I've had a mad crush on my whole life was at your wedding," Sara said. "You have to tell me everything about him. Clearly, you're the sibling I always wanted."

They all laughed.

"We can FaceTime him after dinner to say hi. I missed a call from him last week anyway," Tess replied.

"Uh, that would be amazing. I actually feel myself sweating already," Sara said.

Tess giggled.

"Won't it be kind of late in London?" Jack asked.

"I'm not sure that's where he is, but it doesn't matter. Mick's nocturnal," Tess replied.

"Oh, and Jack said that some rock star once proposed to you, but he doesn't know who it was. We're all dying to find out," Mikey added.

She looked at Jack with wide eyes.

"Omar told me, but he wouldn't name names."

"Well, I'll tell you this much: he's the lead singer in a band and your parents have at least three of their albums on the shelf over there," Tess said, gesturing.

Sara, Julie, and Mikey jumped up so fast they almost knocked over the table.

Tess laughed hysterically.

"Am I going to want to hear this?" Jack asked.

Tess shrugged.

"Oh my God!" Sara screamed. "Jack, this is either going to make you feel very good or very bad about yourself."

Tess laughed uncontrollably, cringing in pain but unable to stop.

Jack leaned over and asked, "How are you doing, sweetheart?"

"Laughter really is the best medicine," she said, putting her hand on his face and kissing him. "But I'm gonna kill Omar."

CHAPTER 9

Mikey, Julie, and the boys left early the next morning. Later that day, Tess and Jack were sitting on the couch drinking coffee when Mary trudged into the house with an armload of grocery bags. "Mom, let me help," Jack said, springing up.

"Thank you, honey," she said. "I bought all the things you said Tess likes."

"Oh, you didn't have to go to that trouble," Tess said.

"Nonsense. It's my pleasure. We're going to take good care of you, just like I promised," Mary said. "Have you eaten yet?"

"No," Tess said.

"I'm going to make you some oatmeal. Jack said that's what you like. This afternoon, I'll make a big pot of vegetable soup. There's nothing like homemade soup when you don't feel well."

"I'd love to help," Tess said.

"You need to rest," Mary said.

"I can sit at the table and chop vegetables or something."

Mary smiled. "We'll see how you feel, dear. Right now, I'm going to fix that oatmeal."

"Let me do it, Mom. I know how she likes it," Jack said.

"All right, honey."

Jack walked over to Tess, kissed the top of her head, and said, "I'll be right back."

"I'll keep Tess company," John said, dropping down into his reclining chair.

Mary unloaded the groceries while Jack made Tess's breakfast. She watched him standing at the stove, faithfully stirring the oatmeal in the pot. "You love her very much," she said.

"More than I could ever say."

She put her hand on his arm. "It makes me so happy to see that you have that kind of lasting love in your life. You're a good man, Jack, and I'm so proud of you. You and Tess are perfect for each other."

That afternoon, Mary announced that she was going to make the soup. Tess insisted that Jack help her to the kitchen so she could lend a hand. He sat her at the table and Mary gave her a cutting board, a knife, and a bunch of celery stalks. Jack touched his forehead to hers and quietly said, "Please take it easy. I'll come back to check on you in a bit."

"Honey, your dad was telling me about the camping trips you all used to take. I never had the chance to tell him about our hiking adventure in Australia. You should go sit with him and tell him about it."

"Okay, sweetheart." He pressed his lips softly to hers.

When he left the room, Mary said, "You wanted to help me so Jack would have time alone with his father."

"Please don't say anything," Tess replied.

Mary smiled. "You know, I was lucky that all three of my children were always good. When Jack was a boy, he was always so quiet, but he was also the sweetest of my children. I thought that sweetness had left him, but I see it again in the way he takes care of you."

"That's who Jack is. He's the kindest, gentlest man I've ever known. He's been like this since the day we met, not only now because I'm injured. He's such a wonderful husband. I didn't think I'd ever get married, but the moment I met him, I knew I had to spend my life with him. I'm so lucky he chose me."

"Tess, I'm awfully sorry that it had to be under these conditions, but John and I are thrilled to have this extra time with you both."

"Sometimes things work out for the best," Tess replied. She held up a celery slice. "Is this how you want them?"

Over the next several days, Jack, John, and Mary continued to care for Tess. Her recovery wasn't without bumps. One afternoon, she reported a bad headache. Jack panicked and implored her to go to the hospital. She begged him not to overreact and asked him to simply call the hospital as a first measure. After reviewing the nature and duration of her headache, her doctor allowed her to monitor it at home. They suggested she take acetaminophen in addition to her ibuprofen, which she did. She took a nap, but Jack was too terrified to leave her side and sat on the edge of the bed the entire time. When she opened her eyes, he rested his hand on her head. "Hi, sweetheart. How are you feeling?"

"Better. My headache is gone."

He started to tear up.

"Were you sitting here the whole time?"

He nodded. "I would never leave you."

"Here," she said, moving over. "Come lie down with me."

He climbed into bed and she curled into him, resting her head on his chest. They interlaced their fingers. "Did you know that this is my favorite thing in the entire world? Just sitting or lying with you, feeling you beside me, touching your hand. I could spend my whole life like this without uttering a single word," she said.

"Me too, baby."

They also had a few embarrassing moments. One afternoon, they were relaxing on the couch while Mary and John tidied the kitchen. Jack leaned over and kissed Tess. Her lips lingered on his, so he pulled her toward him and kissed her passionately. They were making out like teenagers when Mary walked into the room and cleared her throat.

"Uh, I'm sorry to interrupt," she said sheepishly.

"Oh my God. I'm mortified," Tess mumbled.

"Oh, no need dear. I've walked in on Jack doing much worse."

"Mom," Jack whined.

"Sometimes he wasn't even with a girl," Mary teased.

"Mother!" Jack protested. "Yeah, that's not embarrassing."

"But you should take it easy. The doctor said no physical activity, so that includes…"

"I beg you not to finish that sentence," Jack said.

Mary shrugged. "Tess, that reminds me. Would you like to see a family photo album? There's a picture of Jack going to his prom. He tried to grow this little mustache. Just a few whiskers, really. It was precious."

Jack buried his face in his hands and shook his head, moaning dramatically.

Tess giggled. "Why yes, Mary, I would love to see that."

True to form, the events of their Pennsylvania Christmas vacation served as creative fuel for Tess. After a few days cooped up inside, she was itching to breathe the fresh air. One night after dinner, she begged Jack to take her outside on the back deck. Afraid she would slip, he shoveled the deck until it was bone dry, helped her bundle up, and reluctantly took her out. She held his hand and inhaled deeply, looking up at the dark blue sky sparkling with stars.

"It's so beautiful. The night is so clear that we can see all the stars," she said.

"Yeah," he said, wrapping his arms around her.

"I love the stars."

"I know you do, sweetheart."

"Oh look, there's Orion, right over there," she said, pointing. "See that bright blue star near the bottom? That's Rigel, the seventh brightest star in the sky."

Jack smiled. "I see it."

"It's always been my favorite constellation," Tess said, leaning her head against Jack.

"Why?"

"Well, Orion's the hunter. I don't know, there's just something about people seeking; I always wonder if people are seeking something they don't yet have, or something they do have and just don't know it. Like the stars themselves, shining their light long before it reaches us, or the very stardust of which we are made."

He kissed the top of her head.

"It's funny, really. Constellations are just random groups of stars, near each other by happenstance, but they recall something familiar to us, so we see a pattern in the randomness."

They stood staring at the sky, holding each other, no more words spoken until Jack finally said, "I really need to get you off your feet."

"Okay," she whispered, kissing him. "Jack, I need to write."

He walked her back into the house, took off her coat, hat, and boots, and helped her onto the couch. Mary and John were reading in their recliners.

"Can I get you something, dear? Maybe some hot tea?" Mary asked.

"That would be lovely. Thank you," Tess replied. She turned to Jack. "Would you please bring my laptop and reading glasses?"

Jack disappeared upstairs and then returned with the items. She sat on the couch, outstretched her legs, and rested her feet in Jack's lap. She opened her laptop and switched it on. Mary placed her tea on the coffee table and offered her a blanket.

"Thank you," Tess said, looking up.

"Promise me you won't push yourself too hard," Jack said.

"I promise."

She put on her glasses and began typing. More than an hour passed, with Tess only stopping occasionally to take a sip of tea. Eventually, she took her glasses off and placed them on the coffee table.

"What are you working on, sweetheart?" Jack asked.

"When we were outside, I got an idea for my next novel."

"Tess, it's such an honor to see you work. I've been reading your books for nearly twenty years. That you would work on one in my home, well, I don't even know what to say," Mary said.

Tess smiled. "It's only the draft of a beginning, but would you like to read it?"

Mary put her hand on her heart. "Oh Tess, I would love that."

Jack passed his mother the laptop. Tess turned around to lay her head in Jack's lap. He ran his fingers through her hair. "That feels good," she whispered.

When Mary finished reading, her eyes were flooded with tears. "John, please pass me the Kleenex." John handed her a box of tissues and she wiped her face. "Tess, you're a very special person and your talent is singular. You find beauty everywhere, even in the least likely of places. Now I can see that what you really do is connect your experiences to something that connects us all, something language can describe but never name. It runs down to the core. No one else does quite what you do. The pain is laced with infinite hope; that's what lingers." Mary paused to blow her nose. "What you do is extraordinary. The world needs more of it. Thank you for allowing us to be a part of it."

"You're very kind," Tess said, as Jack kissed the side of her head.

***

Although she never brought up the car accident, Tess's act of bravery on Christmas Eve continued to have ripple effects. One day, Mary and John were reading in their recliners and Tess and Jack were snuggling on the sofa, working on a crossword puzzle. The telephone rang. "I'll get it," John said. He walked into the kitchen and returned holding the phone. "Tess, it's for you. It's the chief of police," he said, handing her the receiver.

"Hello? Yes... That really isn't necessary... I see... Okay. Goodbye." She hung up and placed the phone beside her.

She turned to Jack, looking at him like a deer in headlights.

"What is it, Tess?"

"Please help me up." He helped her to her feet. "I'll be right back. I need to get something in our room."

"Sweetheart, let me help you up the stairs."

"I can manage."

They watched as she hobbled slowly upstairs.

After they heard the bedroom door close, John said, "Jack, she looked upset."

"Yeah, I can't imagine what it could be," he replied.

"You should go see what's going on. She really shouldn't try to come back down on her own; she could get hurt," Mary said.

Jack went up to their room. He tapped lightly on the door before walking in. Tess was on the phone. "Please see that she gets the message. Thank you," she said, hanging up.

"Sweetheart, are you all right?"

"I could use a hug," she said quietly.

He put his arms around her, patting the back of her head.

"What's going on?" he whispered.

"It's not important. Let's go back downstairs."

"Okay," he said, kissing her forehead.

Tess clutched her cell phone as Jack helped her back down to the living room sofa. "Everything all right, dear?" Mary asked.

Tess nodded. She picked up the crossword and looked at Jack. "Let's finish it."

Mary and John opened up their books and continued reading. Twenty minutes later, Tess's phone rang.

"Hello? Yes, he's here… Okay."

She put the phone on speaker and placed it on the coffee table. "Madam President, Jack and his parents John and Mary are here with me."

John and Mary sat upright, looking at each other in shock. Jack looked at Tess quizzically.

"Hello, Mr. and Mrs. Miller. Hi, Jack. Your wife is quite the hero," the president said.

"Yes she is, Madam President," Jack replied.

"Tess, I got your message. Are you sure this is something you want me to do?" the president asked.

"Yes. I'm sorry to bother you, but you were the only person I thought could help," Tess replied.

"You know I'd do anything for you, but I wish you'd ask me for something else," the president said.

"Madam President, when I helped you bring Japan and Russia to the table for that arts initiative, you told me privately that you owed me one. I'm calling in that favor now. This is what I want."

"Tess…" the president said.

"Kate, please," Tess said quietly.

"All right. I'll take care of it right away. Jack, are you still there?"

"Yes, Madam President," Jack replied.

"I wanted you on the line because when we get off the phone you should take your wife back to the hospital and have her head examined. We live in a world where people shamelessly vie for credit when they've often done little to deserve it, and Tess, well, I don't know what to say. She's one of a kind."

"I really do appreciate this, Madam President," Tess said.

"Glad to help. Oh, while I have you, I wanted to tell you that I finally had a chance to read *Ray of Light*. It's simply sublime. This was the first time I knew the circumstances that bore one of your novels, and I must say, you truly have an astonishing ability to transform darkness into light. I can't wait to see what this latest adventure inspires," the president said.

"Thank you," Tess replied. "I've already started working on something new."

"I would expect nothing less. I miss you and look forward to seeing you when you're back in DC."

"Jack's mother showed me a wonderful trick for gingersnaps. We'll have to make them next time we're together."

"Can't wait. And Jack, please take good care of my friend," the president said.

"I will," Jack replied.

"Goodbye," the president said.

Tess hung up the phone. Everyone looked at her, dumbfounded and searching for answers. Jack caressed her hand and raised an eyebrow.

"If I tell you, you have to promise not to tell anyone," she said. They all nodded.

"The chief of police called to say that the governor wants to give me some kind of civilian act of heroism award at a public ceremony, which is the last thing I want."

Jack's eyes widened. "So you called the president of the United States to ask her to stop it?"

Tess nodded. "She's the only person I knew who could."

"Oh sweetheart," he said, laughing.

"What?"

"I just love you, that's all," he replied, leaning over to kiss her.

John and Mary looked at each other, their mouths hanging open.

"Tess, I'm really enjoying getting to know you," John said. "May I ask you something?"

"Sure," she replied.

"You radiate kindness and generosity. It seems incredibly important to you that these acts remain private. Why?"

"When we first arrived, you asked about my family. Jack reacted with anger because he was trying to protect me." Jack put his hand on her back and she continued. "The truth is that I had a horrible childhood and survived unspeakable violence."

"We're so sorry, dear," Mary said.

"We're glad you're a part of this family now," John added.

Tess smiled. "I learned at an early age just how important it is to see each person's humanity. The way we treat others is who we become. I've been lucky to travel the world, meeting people from all walks of life, and the lesson has only become clearer. You treat people a certain way simply because they are human, and you are too. There is no other reason. All we have is who we are. When you're famous or successful, it can be challenging because people have all kinds of ideas about you that you can't control. You learn to value the one thing you can control: who you really are. John, you asked why I value anonymity around generosity. All I have is who I am, and I want to be a person who treats people well when no one is looking. I won't allow anyone to take that from me."

John smiled. "Like I said, I'm really enjoying getting to know you. Jack, you did well."

"I know," Jack replied.

Mary said, "Uh, so you're going to make my gingersnaps, dear?"

"I sure am. Remind me, did you lightly pack the brown sugar?" Tess asked.

***

The next day, they were all playing cards when Jack's phone rang.

"Omar's FaceTiming us," he said, swiping to answer the call. "Hey, Omar."

"Hi, Jack. How's our patient doing?"

"She's good, a little better each day. She's even letting me take care of her."

"Wow. I'm impressed. I can't believe you got her to admit she's injured. You know how stubborn she can be."

"I heard that," Tess said. "Where's a pretzel to throw when I need it?"

"Hi, Butterfly. Jack, please put the phone where you can both see it. I'm calling with news."

Jack leaned the phone against a candy dish on the coffee table.

"Omar, I'm glad you called. John is teaching me to play gin rummy. It's really fun," Tess said. "I was telling them about that wild little underground casino Mikhail Petrov took us to in Moscow. Do you remember?"

"How could I forget?" Omar replied.

"What was that card game we were playing, not poker, but the other one?" Tess asked.

"Bloody hell if I know. I think they made it up. They were dropping those gold coins like they were pocket change and chugging that gruesome cherry vodka they were so keen on like it was cola. What I remember most was how the night ended. Nearly turned into a bloody game of Russian roulette when that mafia boss showed up."

"He was in the mafia?" Tess asked. "The short little man with the dark hair who was so kind to me?"

"Butterfly, he was the head of a major crime ring. What did you think was happening when they went to the back room and Mikhail had his goons escort us out?"

"Ha! Well, the whole thing makes more sense now. Anyway, have you ever played gin rummy? I was thinking that we should play more card games on our group game nights when Jack and I are in town."

"That sounds great, Butterfly. Listen, I'm calling with something to share."

"What's up?"

"You know that your Christmas Eve miracle became an international news story, right?"

"Please don't remind me," Tess said with a groan. "I haven't watched television or read a newspaper. Please tell me it's gone away by now."

"Well, yes and no. Are Jack's parents there?"

"Yes," she replied.

"John, what you said to the press outside your home was dignified and brilliant. Well done," Omar said.

"I was glad to help," John replied.

"Well, that clip played around the world," Omar said. "Butterfly, Crystal, Claire, and I were all inundated with messages from your friends and just about everyone in your network. Everyone was begging to know what they could do for you."

"I hope you told them nothing. I'm fine, really. There's no need to make a fuss," Tess said.

"Everyone wanted to reach out to you. I knew you wouldn't want that, but people were insistent on doing something. Clay and I brainstormed and asked ourselves what you would want, and I think we came up with a genius idea. We asked everyone who reached out to make a donation to your favorite charity. We pooled it all. Given how bloody rich your circle is, we suggested a donation of one hundred thousand dollars. Many gave five or even ten times that. Butterfly, there are a lot of very wealthy and powerful people who love you more than you realize. You mean so much to so many people. The list is endless. Mick, Bruce, Paul, I mean everyone. Even those oil tycoons you barely tolerate. They all wanted to contribute on your behalf."

"That's very generous," Tess said.

"Butterfly, brace yourself. We collected over fifty million dollars. It's the largest single donation that organization has ever received."

"What?" she asked softly.

Jack shook his head and put his arm around her.

Mary and John looked at each other with open mouths and sky-high eyebrows.

"Butterfly, I know you acted in the moment without wanting anything in return, as you always do, which is the very reason you're deeply loved by so many. I wanted you to know that your good deed has been multiplied many times over. And don't worry, your name won't be attached. It's all anonymous. I know how your mind works and how this might make you feel, but please remember that sometimes good inspires good and there is only light."

"Omar, I don't know what to say," Tess said, barely audible.

He smiled. "Don't say anything. Please just let Jack and his parents take care of you. We need you healed. I love you beyond measure. Clay loves you too."

"Please express my profound gratitude to everyone. I love you," she said, and they hung up. She turned to Jack, "Did you know about this?"

CHAPTER 9

"No," he replied, scarcely able to get the word out.

John cleared his throat. "Tess, that's the most extraordinary thing I've ever heard."

"What charity is it?" Mary asked.

"Pediatric cancer research," Tess replied.

"For Jack's daughter, Gracie. For our granddaughter," John said softly.

"Yes," she whispered. Her eyes flooded and she began quietly weeping.

"Oh sweetheart, come here," Jack said, embracing her. "It's okay, sweetheart."

She rested her head on his shoulder and cried. A few moments passed and Mary asked, "Is she overcome?"

Jack shook his head. "She's thinking about all the children suffering with cancer, all those suffering right now, and all those who can't be saved." He wiped away Tess's tears. "Is that right, sweetheart?" he whispered.

She nodded, staying firmly pressed to his body.

"Mom, when we first got here, you told Tess that you didn't know how she could write so poignantly about the human experience. This is how. Tess's superpower is compassion. She feels people's pain and suffering as if it were her own. She cares about everyone."

"Such a kind soul," Mary said, taking a tissue from her pocket to wipe her eyes.

Jack continued holding Tess, caressing her head. "This will help a lot of people, sweetheart. It means so much to me. I love you with my whole heart, forever," he whispered.

Tess pulled back. She kissed him and said, "Can we please just play cards?"

Everyone nodded.

Soon, it was New Year's Eve. Tess and Jack decided that she was well enough to travel, and they wanted to be in their home to ring in the new year. They planned to spend two nights in DC and then go to Hawaii where the warm climate would make Tess's recovery easier. They both hugged Mary and John for ages and promised to return for Easter, when Tess would happily do a reading at the local library. "We're so glad you're a part of this family," Mary whispered to Tess.

"We love you both," John said.

Jack took Tess's hand and they headed home, carrying the Millers in their hearts.

CHAPTER 10

"Welcome home, sweetheart," Jack said, as they walked through their front door. Jack helped Tess to the living room couch and then instructed the driver to leave the luggage in the foyer. After locking up, he took the seat beside her. "How are you doing?"

"I'm glad to be home," she said. He rubbed her earlobe and played with her hair as she spoke. "On the jet I was thinking about something Omar said at Shelby's when we all got together after Thanksgiving. He said he was scared during college, not knowing where he'd end up or how he'd survive. Do you remember?"

Jack nodded. "He said you didn't seem to have that same fear."

"I guess it's because I never really had something that felt like a home, so I hadn't lost anything like he had. When he came out to his parents during his freshman year of college, he knew they would sever all ties with him. He loved them and had many happy childhood memories. Losing them was agony. Having nowhere to call home was agony. It still hurts him, all these years later. Even though he's the most upbeat, cheerful person I know, he carries deep wells of pain. It's something that's always connected us. But for me, I didn't even know what it would feel like to have a real home, somewhere safe, somewhere I wanted to be, somewhere to hang holiday decorations or toast the new year."

"You will never have to feel that way again," he said.

"I know. Now there are so many places that feel like home to me: here in DC, our home in Maui, your parents' house, anywhere you are."

He leaned forward and gently kissed her.

"Thank you for taking care of me," she said.

"Sweetheart, you never have to thank me for that. How do you feel? Maybe you could use a nap."

She shook her head. "I'm okay."

"Well, let me get your meds and then we can figure out how to ring in the new year. I'm thinking a movie and takeout of your choice."

She smiled. "Sounds perfect. But honey, please help me up."

He helped her up and she retrieved her laptop bag, unzipped it, and pulled out Genevieve's drawing. She hung it on the refrigerator with a rainbow heart magnet. Jack came up behind her, wrapped his hands around her waist, and they stood for a moment, examining the drawing.

"Some people will never know just how special it is to have someplace to hang mementos," she said.

He kissed the top of her head. "I know you don't like to talk about it, but it's just us. What you did for that little girl, I don't even have the words."

She turned to face him. "Jack, did it make you think of Gracie?"

"Yes," he muttered.

"Was it hard for you, that it was someone else's daughter who was saved?"

"Yes."

"I'm so sorry," she said, putting her hand on his cheek.

He took her hand, kissed it softly, and said, "Come on, sweetheart, you need to take your pills."

***

"Can I please have a summer roll?" Tess asked.

Jack put one on her plate. "Here's the peanut sauce," he said, handing her a small container.

"Thank you, baby. This is the perfect New Year's Eve: just you and me, Thai food, and a movie in the place we got married."

He smiled. "Okay, so what are we watching? It's your choice."

"I picked dinner, you can choose the movie."

"Oh, you may live to regret that."

"Whatever you want is fine with me, even one of those killing spree monstrosities."

"As much fun as it is to watch you close your eyes and ask me to tell you when a scene is over, I say we go for a comedy and start the year with laughter."

They watched *The Out-of-Towners* and spent the next hour and a half eating and laughing uproariously. When the movie ended, Jack cleaned up and gave Tess her medication.

"Sweetheart, I know you like to stay up until midnight, but you really need some rest."

"Okay," she said.

"Wow, you're not even going to give me a hard time?"

"What can I say? I like it when you take care of me."

He smiled and took her hand. They walked to their room and got ready for bed.

"Let me help you into bed," Jack said.

"Jack, will you dance with me?"

"Sweetheart, you're supposed to stay off your feet."

"Just one song. Our song. Please."

He kissed her forehead. "Okay, baby. One song."

"Dim the lights," she said.

He grabbed his phone and put on "All of Me." He took her in his arms, one hand on the small of her back, and they slowly swayed, melting into each other. When the song ended, they kissed each other tenderly.

"We haven't made love in over a week," she whispered. "It's the longest we've ever gone."

"I know, baby. But you need to heal. It will be a few more weeks."

"Don't you miss being with me?"

"Tess, making love with you is pure ecstasy. You're so beautiful in every way. When we're together and I get to be with you like that, I feel like the luckiest person alive. I don't always have the words like you do, so what I love most is showing you how I feel about you."

She pulled his head to her and kissed him.

"But even if we were never able to be like that again, I would still feel like the luckiest man in the world. All I want is to be with you. I'm not taking any chances. I'm not risking anything happening to you."

"We can kiss," she said.

He caressed her cheek, picked her up carefully, and put her on the bed. He turned off the lights, lay beside her, pulled the blanket onto them, and started kissing her. He kissed her lightly and she reciprocated, each cradling the other's face in their hands. They kissed for ages. When they finally parted, Tess whispered, "I love you more than words."

"I love you so much, sweetheart."

She looked down and began to tear up.

"Hey, what's this?" he asked, gently brushing away her tears. "Are you in pain?"

"No, it's not that. It's just…"

"What, baby?"

She looked at him and quietly said, "I feel so guilty and I don't want to start the new year this way."

"What could you possibly have to feel guilty about?"

"It's just that you're such a wonderful husband and you're always so good to me and…"

He pulled her closer to him and tucked her hair behind her ear.

"Jack, every minute we've been together, I've always known how you feel about me. But for the first two years of our marriage, once in a while when we weren't together, if you were at work or something, I would wonder about whether or not you really loved me. It's not because of anything you did. It's me. There's something wrong with me. I feel so ashamed," she said, tears sliding down her cheeks.

"Shh," he whispered, wiping the tears away. He placed a delicate kiss on her lips. "There's nothing wrong with you. You're perfect exactly as you are. You have nothing to be ashamed about. Everyone feels insecure sometimes."

"Do you?" she asked.

"You saw what happened at my parents' house. I was overwhelmed by insecurity. And Tess, not a moment goes by that I don't realize you could have any man you want."

"I only want you."

"I know, baby. I know how you feel about me. Rock stars, royals, the wealthiest businessmen in the world, they've all pursued you, but you chose me. So of course there have been moments when I wondered how I got so lucky. I'm only human. But I feel emboldened by your love; you make me feel strong. Still, I know that if I ever screw this up, there will be a long line of very impressive men waiting in the wings."

"You could never mess it up. I could never be with anyone else after you. I'm completely in love with you."

"And I'm completely in love with you. Do you ever feel that way now, like you're not sure about how I feel?"

"No, never. I promise."

He kissed her tenderly. "Good. All I want is for you to feel safe and loved, like how you make me feel. I love you with my whole heart, forever."

She looked down and bit her lip.

"Sweetheart, is there something else?"

"Yes," she said faintly.

"What, baby?"

"It's just something I thought about at Christmas dinner with your family. I didn't want to say anything when we were staying there, and after all you've done for me, I feel silly bringing it up, but I'm afraid if I don't it will undo me."

He caressed her arm. "I always want you to tell me what's going on in your mind."

"Jack, you know how I feel about your service to this country. I admire you so much. Your patriotism, well, it's not a sentiment I've ever really felt. I've always thought of myself more as a citizen of the world. I love how much you love this country and I'm humbled by your sacrifice, so I don't want you to misunderstand, but…"

"What, baby? You can tell me anything."

"Your family is so wonderful. Anyone would love them. And at Christmas dinner, when I saw the way you interacted with Mikey and Sara, the closeness between all of you, and how much you love your parents, I realized for the first time just how much you've sacrificed. It couldn't have been easy to let them go. Yet you were able to do it, to make the choice to leave them because of something you felt called to do. I know you love me, but…"

"Oh sweetheart, no. I'm never going to leave you, not for anything, not ever. I love you so much."

"I know, but Jack, I could see how much you love them. It must have been torture walking away. Yet somehow, you did."

"There are a couple of things you need to understand. First, I was very young when I joined the military and started down that path. I didn't realize where it would lead at the time. Once I was in that impossible position, I felt there was no other choice but to let them go. Second, and most importantly, the day we got married, I made a lifelong commitment to you. Do you remember my vows?"

"Yes. You said you'd give me the same level of commitment that you had given to serving this country."

"That's right. For so many years, I had given one hundred percent of my effort and heart and loyalty to service. The day we got married, I made the decision to give you that commitment instead. I don't take that promise lightly. Tess, your happiness is my top priority. I'm completely dedicated to you and our marriage, above all else. I always will be. It was my choice and it's the best choice I've ever made."

She smiled brightly.

He leaned forward and pressed his lips to hers.

"I'm sorry. It just popped into my mind and I've been unable to shake it," she said softly.

"Don't be sorry. It's understandable and I always want you to tell me how you feel. Do you feel better?"

"Yes, baby. Thank you. There's just one more thing."

"What, sweetheart?"

"You've never asked me to change in any way. You've always accepted me the way I am, and I need you to know I would never want you to give up any part of yourself for me. When I met your family, I realized just how much serving this country means to you. I hope you don't feel you've sacrificed who you are to be with me."

He smiled. "Not at all. I love the life we've built. My work still satisfies me, in some ways even more now because you've given me the freedom to choose how to serve, and I get to be your husband every day. I'm happier than I ever thought was possible, and I haven't sacrificed a single iota of myself; I am my truest self when I am with you."

"Good. Because I want to be your wife forever and always."

He pressed a long, tender kiss onto her lips. "Sweetheart, I can't wait to wake up in the new year with you in my arms, and every day after that. Forever and always."

***

"Hey," Tess whispered, the morning sunlight on her face.

"Good morning, sweetheart," Jack said, curling up beside her. "Happy New Year."

"Happy New Year."

"How are you feeling?"

"A little better. Happy. Happy to be here with you. Happy to be home."

"Me too."

"What time is it?" she asked.

"We must have been tired; it's nearly ten. We need to get up and get ready."

"What's the rush?" she asked.

"I have a surprise for you."

"You do? What is it?"

"You'll see. Just promise me one thing: you'll remember that you're still recovering and you need to take it easy. I don't want you to overdo it."

She nodded. "Promise."

Jack got out of bed and reached for Tess's hand. "Let me help you get ready and then I'll go make coffee."

"I think I can shower myself. Maybe you could just put my clothes on the bed."

He kissed her forehead. "Okay, sweetheart, but if you need me, just holler. Don't forget to take your meds; they're on the nightstand."

An hour later, Tess meandered into the kitchen. "Hey, sweetheart. How'd it go?"

"Okay. Easier in our own home."

"Here, let me help you onto the couch."

"I can do it, Jack."

"I know, but it'll be gentler on your body if I help you. Please, sweetheart."

She smiled. "Okay, baby. Thank you."

He lent a hand as she sat on the couch. "Want some coffee?"

"Yes, please," she said.

He brought her a mug and said, "I need to take a quick shower. Do you need anything before I go?"

"Yeah, I need a kiss."

He leaned down and gave her a soft peck.

"Now I'm perfect," she said.

"Wait right here. I'll be back in a flash and then it will be time for your surprise."

Tess sipped her coffee and sorted through the mail that had piled up while they'd been away. Before she had finished her first cup of coffee, Jack returned. "Anything good in the mail?" he asked.

"All junk, unless you see value in four takeout menus from the same place. So, what's my surprise?"

"I know how much you miss Omar and everyone," he said.

"Are they coming over?" she asked, her face lighting up with a hopeful smile.

"Omar and Clay will be here any minute. I thought you could use some time with just them. Joe, Bobby, and Gina are coming in about an hour. I think Joe's bringing Luciana, so we'll finally get to meet her. They're all bringing food, a vegetarian potluck in your honor. But remember, you promised you'd take it easy."

"Come here," she said, pulling his hand.

He sat beside her and she ran her fingers through his hair. "That's the best surprise. I can't think of a better way to start the new year. Thank you."

"I know you expected to have more time with everyone this winter, and now we're going back to Maui tomorrow, so I thought..."

She leaned forward and kissed him passionately. "Thank you, baby."

Just then, the doorbell rang.

"Jack, I want to get up," Tess said.

He helped her stand and then went to answer the door.

"Hey, Omar. Hey, Clay," he said. "Wow, looks like you brought a feast."

"There's actually still a pastry box and carton of chilled champagne in the car," Clay said.

"Give me your key and I'll grab it," Jack said.

Omar and Clay each set a large casserole dish on the bar and then Omar sprinted over to Tess. "Oh Butterfly, I've never been happier to see anyone than I am to see you. Can I hug you gently?"

Smiling through the tears in her eyes, she opened her arms and they embraced.

"Don't let me hurt you," Omar whispered.

"You could never," she whispered.

Eventually, Clay said, "Hey, I want some of that."

Tess laughed, and she and Clay hugged. "Thank God you're all right. I love you," Clay said.

"I love you too," she replied.

Tess and Omar curled up on the couch, inseparable. They blabbered on a mile a minute as Jack and Clay watched them from across the room and grinned. An hour later, Bobby and Gina arrived with a tray of Italian baked eggplant.

"Tess, I'm so glad you're okay," Bobby said, hugging her softly. "We were so worried."

"I'm fine, really. It was so sweet of you guys to call and text each day."

"I've always known you're a badass, but throwing yourself in front of a car? We need you in one piece, okay? Leave the hero stuff to us," he said.

She laughed.

Joe and Luciana arrived shortly after with a huge platter of homemade potato empanadas.

"Is it safe to hug you?" Joe asked.

"Always," Tess said.

"You are one brave woman. Thank God you're okay. We were all worried. Jack was a wreck," he said.

"He's been taking very good care of me," she replied.

"Uh, yes, and Butterfly, I'm a bit hurt. I've never even been able to get you to admit that you're sick or injured, let alone convince you to take care of yourself," Omar said.

"If it's any consolation, I didn't have much of a choice this time. A car hit me."

Omar laughed. "Well, then I won't take it personally."

"Everyone, this is Luciana," Joe said.

They all said hello and made introductions. "It's so wonderful to meet you," Tess said.

"Joe has told me so much about all of you. He said you're a writer," Luciana said.

"Ha! I like you already," Tess replied with a smile.

"Actually, he told me to say that. I've read all of your books," Luciana said bashfully.

"Well, I'll try not to hold that against you," Tess replied.

Luciana smiled. "You're very talented and I'm always happy to meet another artist."

"Yes, I hear you're a gifted sculptor. I would love to learn about your work."

"How about everyone helps themselves to some food, I'll pour the bubbly, and we can sit in the living room and catch up," Jack suggested. He put his hand on Tess's back. "Sweetheart, let me help you get situated and then I'll fix you a plate."

"Okay, baby. I want a little bit of everything."

"Just sparkling water for me, please," Gina said.

Everyone looked at her in surprise.

"Go ahead, tell them," Bobby said.

"We're expecting!" she announced, beaming. "I'm in my second trimester, so we figured that it's safe to start telling people."

"Oh wow, congratulations!" Jack exclaimed.

"That's wonderful news," Joe added.

"Oh Gina, I'm so happy for you two," Tess said, tears in her eyes.

Gina walked over and hugged her. "After the way you helped me through my miscarriage, I couldn't wait to tell you most of all."

"I knew it would happen for you," Tess whispered. "You're going to be a wonderful mother."

When they all sat down with their food, Jack passed around flutes of champagne and sparkling water for Tess and Gina. He sat beside Tess, raised his glass, and said, "Let's toast to being together with the people we love and to a very happy and healthy new year."

"Cheers!"

"Salud!"

"Omar, do you realize the next time we all raise a toast will be at your wedding?" Tess said.

Omar grinned from ear to ear.

"That is, if Clay doesn't get cold feet first. I mean, who could blame him?" Tess said.

"Oh, how I missed you, Butterfly."

"Just don't let him get drunk," Clay joked. "I don't want him claiming he was incapacitated and trying to get out of it."

"Well, that's a relief. I thought you'd be the one who was more likely to look for a loophole," Omar jested.

"I can't think of a better way to celebrate Valentine's Day than watching you two take your vows," Tess said.

"Bloody hell, Butterfly, I know you had a near death whatever, but it's brunch. Lighten up," Omar said, laughing.

Tess giggled.

"I'm just teasing. It means so much to me and Clay that you will all be there to celebrate with us," Omar said.

"Cheers," Tess said, raising her glass.

"On that note, let's dig in," Jack said.

"Clay, you were so sweet to make the baked pumpkin. It's amazing," Tess said.

Clay smiled. "I know it's your favorite."

"And Luciana, these empanadas are delicious," Tess said.

"You can fill them with anything. I can teach you how to make them some time if you like."

"I would love that. I've heard that you've gotten Joe to go dancing with you. I'm impressed."

"He's getting pretty good, now that I've gotten him to loosen up," Luciana said.

Joe blushed.

"I love to dance. There's a great bar not far from here that plays salsa music. Maybe you and Jack can come with us sometime," Luciana said.

"I like you more and more by the minute. I love to dance. Jack will only dance to slow songs, but maybe we can work on him," Tess said, rubbing Jack's arm.

"The women are ganging up on us, Joe," Jack said.

"Don't fight it. It's a lost cause," Joe said.

They all laughed.

They spent the next two hours eating, drinking, talking, and laughing. Eventually, Omar said, "Butterfly, I hate to miss even a second with you, but we're under strict orders from Jack to make sure you take it easy. Perhaps we should clean everything up and get going so you can rest."

"Okay," she said. "I'm having so much fun, but I am a little tired."

"We'll all be together again soon, in Maui no less, and I'm still holding out hope that you'll wear a grass skirt and impress us with your belly dancing skills," Omar said.

"I wouldn't hold your breath," Tess said.

Everyone cleaned up, leaving enough food for Tess and Jack to eat for dinner that night, and wrapping the rest of the leftovers to take with them. They all hugged and said how they couldn't wait to see each other in Hawaii.

Once the house was empty, Tess slipped her hands around Jack's waist. "That was the best New Year's Day we could have had. Thank you."

"Nothing makes me happier than seeing you happy," he said, taking her face in his hands and kissing her.

"I love you so much," she said.

"I love you too, sweetheart. You need to take your meds, and then I think you should lie down and rest a little."

"Will you come with me?"

"There's nowhere else I'd be."

Jack helped Tess to bed. They spent the rest of the day snuggling, watching movies, and eating leftovers. The next day, they flew to Hawaii.

CHAPTER 11

Tess and Jack quickly settled into life at their Hawaiian retreat. Tess was happy to be in the warm climate where she could wear lighter, more comfortable clothing and easily walk around outdoors, soaking up the sunshine and ocean air. Jack continued to care for her, taking every precaution for a smooth recovery. Every few days, he rode the bike into town and returned with a bag of fresh food. He waited on Tess hand and foot, making her tropical smoothie bowls in the morning, fruit and vegetable salads in the afternoon, and grilled feasts for dinner.

Their loved ones routinely texted, called, and FaceTimed to check on Tess. Mikey and Julie bought into the medical supplies company and called to tell them all about it. Joe FaceTimed from an art show that included some of Luciana's work. He moved the phone around the room so Tess and Jack could see all of her beautiful sculptures. When they hung up, Jack commented that what he noticed most was the smile plastered across Joe's face. Bobby and Gina emailed them a picture of their first sonogram, and Tess was so happy for them that she cried. No one called more frequently than Omar. He and Tess often spent hours on the phone, talking and laughing until one of their batteries died. Sometimes Clay would pop in to say hello, settle an argument, or join in with Tess as she teased Omar.

In the beginning, Tess wrote for a couple of hours each morning while Jack went for a run or devoted some time to his consulting or volunteer work. They typically spent the rest of the day lounging by the pool. When Tess was able to make it safely down the precarious stairs to the beach, they spent many days in their seaside cabana, watching the waves roll in and out and splashing around in the salt water, which Tess found immeasurably healing. As the weeks passed, Tess's bruises turned from dark purple, to light purple, to green, to yellow, and she spent more and more time writing. Exactly four weeks after her accident, she sat on their veranda, finishing a mouthwatering dinner Jack had prepared.

"You've spoiled me so much, baby," Tess said.

He took her hand. "You deserve only good things. I love taking care of you. I'm going to bring the dishes into the kitchen."

Jack cleaned up while Tess looked out at the ocean and sky, cobalt touching cobalt. Soon, Jack returned.

"It's so clear tonight. Let's look at the stars," she said.

They walked hand in hand to the edge of the balcony. Jack stood behind Tess, slipping his arms around her waist.

"Wow, it's amazing tonight," she said, looking up at the endless sky bursting with stars. "Did you know that in Hawaii, you can see over eighty-five percent of the stars that are visible from earth?"

He smiled. "No, but that must be why you love it here so much. I do know that you can clearly see both the North Star and the Southern Cross."

"It's so incredible to think that we are really just stardust. When you stand here and see how vast everything is, how small we are, it seems like a miracle that two people ever find their way to each other."

"I think some things are just meant to be," he said. "There's no rhyme or reason, other than it's destined to be. The universe conspires to make it happen, and it's our job to not screw it up. I can't imagine spending my life without you. We had to find each other."

She turned to face him. He put his hand on the back of her head, his fingers woven into her hair, and kissed her tenderly. They gazed back into the starry darkness.

"Oh wow, look, a shooting star," Tess said.

Jack tightened his grip on her waist.

"I spent years wishing on make-believe shooting stars that I'd have a safe home and feel love, true love. Never once did I dream it would feel this good."

He put his hands on her shoulders and turned her toward him. "I'll never be able to tell you what you mean to me," he said.

"You can show me. Let's go to bed," she said.

They strolled to their room and Tess said, "Wait here." She disappeared into their master bathroom and reemerged a few minutes later wearing a white lace teddy.

"Wow, you are so beautiful."

She wrapped her arms around his neck and pressed her body against his. "It's been so long I feel like it's our wedding night. Be with me, Jack."

He cupped her face in his hands and kissed her slowly, deepening his kisses at her passionate response. "Jack," she whispered, "I've missed you." He picked her up, carried her to the bed, and lay her down, then quickly pulled off his own clothes. He admired her body lying on the bed and hesitated, his sculpted muscles quivering with tension. She slid the strap of her negligee off her shoulder and reached for his hand. "Jack, I need you. All of you." He climbed into bed and they made love tenderly, screaming in bliss, and then rested in each other's arms.

"Are you okay?" Jack asked.

"I've never been better."

"I love you so much, Tess. I love you with my whole heart, forever."

"I love you more than anything," she said.

They slept with their bodies entwined, and when they awoke the next morning, they made love again.

CHAPTER 12

The car service dropped Bobby, Gina, Joe, and Luciana at the estate in the late afternoon of February twelfth. They all raved about flying on Tess's jet. Tess gave them the grand tour, and then Jack directed both couples to their rooms in the guesthouse. After unpacking, they all convened outside on the lanai. They were catching up when Omar and Clay arrived, after checking into their hotel suite.

"Tess, the tropical flowers in our hotel room are spectacular. Thank you so much," Clay said as they embraced.

"It was our pleasure," Tess replied. "We want everything to be perfect for you two."

Omar smiled. "It's sublime, Butterfly," he said, hugging her. "The suite is extraordinary."

"You deserve every happiness." She turned to the group. "Well, I promised Omar lots of fruity drinks with paper umbrellas, so it's cocktail time! Who wants a mai tai?"

They sat on the veranda, watching the sunset and enjoying a light dinner. They made plans to take an early hike the next day to a nearby waterfall before it got too hot, and then they retired for the evening.

The next morning, a van brought them to the trailhead of a famous path through the jungle that lead to a spectacular oasis. Bobby was concerned about Gina making the trip, but she insisted on going. Tess and Jack assured him it was a short, easy hike, and that they could rest whenever she needed. In his element, Jack guided them down the trail, pointing out uneven spots where someone could trip. When they arrived at their destination, they couldn't believe their eyes.

"Well, here we are. This is one of our favorite spots on the island," Tess said, rubbing Jack's arm.

"It's breathtaking," Omar said, looking at the pool of aqua water as clear as glass, surrounded by cliffs covered in lush greenery and an enormous, roaring waterfall.

Clay put his arm around Omar as they admired the exquisite scene.

"It's nirvana," Luciana said, taking Joe's hand. Joe smiled and kissed her cheek.

Gina looked at Bobby and said, "I'm so glad I didn't miss this."

"Me too, babe," he said, pecking her cheek and then rubbing her belly.

"Well, you know what they say about the last one in," Tess said, shimmying out of her clothes to reveal a turquoise bikini. Everyone followed her lead. As they splashed in the water, Tess swam to the base of a cliff and scaled the side, ready to jump in.

As they watched, Omar leaned toward Jack and asked, "Uh, is that safe?"

"She always does it, over and over again. It's pretty safe. You know Tess – she's fearless," he said, a proud smile across his face.

"I must say, although this makes me nervous, it's wonderful to see her healthy again," Omar said.

"It sure is," Jack said.

When Tess landed in the water with a massive splash, she sprang up laughing and swam over to the group.

"You have quite a reckless streak, don't you, Butterfly?" Omar said.

"Oh please. My biggest fear is losing my bathing suit bottom. That actually happened to me once. Jack looked all around, but he couldn't find it."

Jack leaned over and whispered, "I didn't try very hard."

She patted his chest. "Come on, baby, give me a kiss."

They kissed and then Tess looked at Omar and said, "Don't be a wimp. You're marrying a surgeon, after all. If things go awry, he can always patch you up."

Omar rolled his eyes and opened his mouth to respond, but was interrupted when Bobby and Gina waded over.

When Tess saw Gina in her bathing suit, she noticed a growing baby bump. "Oh look, Gina! You're starting to show," she said.

"I can feel it fluttering around," Gina replied, glowing.

Bobby put his hand on her stomach. "It's so cool."

Tess smiled and pulled Jack's hand, leading him away from the group. When they were off in a quiet spot near the waterfall, he put his hands on her hips. "You're so gorgeous," he said, leaning in to kiss her. He moved from her lips, to her neck, to her ear.

"Baby, if you keep doing that, we're going to need more privacy than we have here," she said.

He kissed her slowly, draped his arms around her, and said, "This is really paradise."

"The best part is being here with all of them. Look how happy they are. Everyone's so in love," she said.

They watched their friends, smiles across their faces for the bliss of the moment. When everyone grew tired of swimming, they put their clothes on. Before leaving, they turned to take a final look at their magical oasis.

"Look, there's a rainbow," Omar said.

"It's funny how putting different colors together suddenly turns them into something else, something more spectacular than they would ever be on their own," Tess said.

"Always the writer, my dramatic little Butterfly," Omar joked.

Tess smiled. "Perhaps the rainbow is good luck."

"Perhaps," Omar said, grabbing Tess's hand and pulling her to him for a hug.

"Okay, follow me," Jack said, leading the way.

They smiled, holding onto the ones they loved, and headed back to the estate. They spent the rest of the day snacking on an endless supply of fresh tropical fruits, cheese, and crackers, and lounging at the pool and beach.

After a day of sunshine, they were all relaxed and ready to break bread.

***

Tess set the outdoor dining table while Jack prepared dinner. Omar and Clay happily elected themselves the bartenders; Omar made pineapple, coconut, and rum drinks in the blender, which he called "Paradise's Nectar," while Clay added a little paper umbrella to each glass. They all enjoyed grilled red snapper plucked from the sea that morning, homemade black bean burgers, and an assortment of grilled vegetables and fruits as they watched the sky turn from light blue to pink to coral to starry darkness.

They were chatting and laughing when Omar quietly said, "I can't believe I'm getting married tomorrow."

"That's not cold feet, is it?" Clay asked.

"Far from it. It's just that I didn't think I'd ever get married. You know how it is when you grow up gay, you don't necessarily dare to even dream it, certainly not in my house," Omar replied.

"Besides, for a long time it was unclear if someone would actually *want* to marry him," Tess said with a giggle. "You're a brave man, Clay."

"That was cold, Tess. Good one, though," Omar said, raising his glass. "Of course, not everyone gets proposals left and right like you, Butterfly. You certainly left a long trail of broken hearts, and dare I say, more than a few shattered egos."

Tess rolled her eyes. "I've never been serious about anyone until Jack. Luckily for me, he felt the same."

Jack smiled and blew her a kiss.

"Well, of course you haven't taken Jack down memory lane. If he only knew about your epic brush-offs, and you do have some doozies. She would have scared you off," Omar said.

"Nothing would have stopped me from wanting Tess. I would have asked her to marry me every day until she said yes," Jack said.

"I see you've trained him well, Butterfly," Omar said.

"I wish I had something to throw at you," Tess rebuffed.

Omar laughed.

"We should all tell our best or funniest breakup stories," Bobby said.

"Ooh, good idea. Tomorrow, we're celebrating the ones that last; tonight, let's pay homage to those that did not," Omar said.

"You're twisted," Clay said.

"He is," Tess agreed.

"I have one," Luciana said.

"Do I want to hear this?" Joe asked.

Luciana smiled.

"Lay it on us," Bobby said.

"It was a first date. We met online. He wanted to take me to dinner, and I suggested a little Mediterranean place in my neighborhood. Halfway through our meal, he excused himself and went to the men's room. Forty minutes later, he still hadn't come back. I assumed he ditched me, so I paid the bill and left. The next day, he left me a voicemail saying he'd been sick in the bathroom, and then he asked me out again."

"Oh my God, that's terrible," Gina said, giggling.

"He must have been so embarrassed," Jack said. "I can't believe he called you."

"I warned him not to order those grape leaves. They always seemed a little off there," Luciana said.

They all laughed.

"Did you call him back?" Joe asked.

Luciana shook her head. "I felt badly, but I'm a believer in kismet and passion. If that's how the first date goes, it doesn't bode well for the future. I didn't know what to say that wouldn't make it worse, so I didn't return his call."

"Well, it worked out for me," Joe said, putting his arm around her.

Everyone smiled.

"Mine is short and simple," Bobby said. "It was in high school. I was dating a girl who had a twin sister and I got them confused in a major way. Major. Let me tell you, there's no coming back from that."

They all laughed.

"No, man, I can't imagine how you can recover from that," Jack said.

"Dude, you can't," Bobby said emphatically, taking a swig of his cocktail.

"I have a funny one," Gina said. "Well, it's kind of humiliating, actually."

"Ooh, I can't wait," Bobby said.

Gina playfully hit his arm. "The abridged version is that the guy was on a date with me and another woman at the same time."

They all laughed.

"Uh, exactly how did he even manage that?" Bobby asked.

"We were at a big, crowded club. We were sitting on stools at the end of the bar. He'd hang out with me and then disappear for like twenty minutes at a time. Eventually, I got up to look for him. He had a table with another woman on the other side of the place."

"Was it your first date?" Bobby asked.

She shook her head. "It was our third. It was his second date with the other woman."

"Holy shit, that's too much," Bobby said, erupting into laughter.

Gina hit his arm again.

"Wow, what a jerk," Tess said.

"Before you get too judgmental, Butterfly, don't forget what they say about those in glass houses," Omar said.

"You did that?" Jack asked, his eyes wide. "You booked two guys at the same time?"

"Of course not, never," she replied.

"Oh, what Tess did was much better. I suspect their egos are still bruised, all these years later. This is actually the story of a double breakup, two birds, one stone, as they say."

"Please, someone, get me something I can throw," Tess quipped.

"Actually, now that I think about it, it was actually a triple dump. Your leading man ditched his model of the moment for you," Omar said.

"You're just the worst," Tess said, shaking her head.

"Are you going to tell them, or should I?" Omar asked.

"I don't think Jack wants to hear it. It's bad enough you told him about a certain singer I was involved with," Tess replied. "You're terrible at keeping secrets."

"Oh, I think Jack will want to hear this one. It involves Tess, a movie director, and Hollywood's most eligible bachelor," Omar said.

"You were with a movie star?" Jack asked.

Tess shrugged. "Well, I wouldn't say *with*."

"Yeah, I definitely want to hear this," Jack said.

"Uh, yeah. We all do," Bobby added with a laugh.

"I think the consensus is clear," Omar said.

"You're terrible," Tess replied.

"We were in the south of France. Tess was attending the Cannes Film Festival on the arm of a director. I wasn't there for the first dumping, or the old switcheroo as they say, so hopefully Tess will fill us in on the missing details. What I do know is that she went with the director and left with the movie star."

"The director was more interesting," Tess muttered.

Omar laughed. "Not just any old movie star, but Hollywood's most eligible bachelor, known for his weakness for blonde super models and his unrelenting bachelor status."

Gina's eyes were wide. "You don't mean…"

"Don't you say his name," Tess warned.

"Let's just call him Theo," Omar said.

"Oh my God!" Gina exclaimed, leaping from her seat.

"Easy there, you're carrying my baby," Bobby said.

"I hate you," Tess said to Omar.

"Love you too, Butterfly," Omar replied. "So anyway, I'm not entirely sure what happened, but Tess went with the director and left with Theo. The next thing I know, she's calling me at the hotel to tell me she's on his yacht and isn't sure when she'll be back."

"I'm going to interrupt you right there. That director spent the entire night schmoozing, trying to work the room and get financing for his next picture. You know how I feel about people who mix business and pleasure. That's no way to treat your date."

Omar laughed. "So tell us, how did Theo sweep you off your feet?"

She shrugged. "I was bored and he started talking to me. He seemed to become infatuated very quickly. I called him out for being there with another woman but spending his time with me. He asked me to wait and then walked over to her and ended it then and there, right next to the cold seafood buffet. Honestly, I couldn't believe it. I wasn't even interested in him, but after that, he said I owed him at least one drink, which naturally he wanted to have on his yacht. The whole thing made me laugh. I must admit, he can be quite charming."

"Oh my God, I'm seriously living vicariously through you. He's so gorgeous," Gina said.

"Uh, again, carrying my kid," Bobby said, taking a swill of his drink.

Gina laughed and playfully smacked his arm again. "Go on, Tess. Tell us more."

"Yes, do go on Tess, because I was there for the last bit and it was the stuff of legend," Omar said.

"Oh please, it was nothing. We spent a few days on his yacht, that was it."

"And there are paparazzi pictures to prove it," Omar said, laughing.

"Really?" Jack asked.

Omar nodded. "You can probably Google it. The paps took loads of photos of the two of them sunbathing on the boat. Tess was wearing an enormous hat to protect her skin, being that she is the fairest in all the land."

"You're too much," Tess said.

"They were splashed across the cover of every magazine, but you can't really see who Tess is unless you know her. Poor guy, by the time the pictures hit newsstands, she had dumped him," Omar said. "And in the most iconic possible way, I might add."

"What happened?" Jack asked.

"He told me I was the only woman he could imagine tying himself to. It was a bit ludicrous since we had only known each other for a few days. Honestly, he seemed to mostly be interested in what women look like. He went on and on about the beautiful models he'd been with and tired of, as if it were some sort of accomplishment. I think he was looking for something more, at least momentarily. He said he would have everything with me: beauty, brains, and talent, in his ridiculous words. But I don't think he had any real interest in being with someone who was his equal."

"Butterfly, you weren't his equal. You were much better than him."

"I know. I came to the same conclusion."

Jack laughed.

"You could have been Amal Clooney, you know, before there was an Amal Clooney. Such a trendsetter," Omar said, shaking his head for effect.

Tess giggled. "Anyway, he was talking about sailing to Saint-Tropez or somewhere. I told him I needed to go to my hotel to talk with Omar and think about it. Then I picked up Omar; we had this wonderful little red convertible I had rented."

"Bloody hell, that was scary. God, she's a bad driver. The roads on those cliffs are no joke, either. I'm amazed we lived to tell the tale."

"She is a terrible driver," Jack agreed.

"Hey!" she said, "You're supposed to be on my side."

"I am, but sweetheart, you're an awful driver."

"Well, just remember I have spent most of my adult life with drivers taking me all over. I haven't had as much practice as some people," Tess said.

"When we first came to Hawaii, Tess wanted to drive the Harley. I thought, 'Holy shit, we'll end up splattered on the road,'" Jack said, erupting into laughter.

"I still want to drive it," Tess protested.

"Sweetheart, how about you try to master four wheels before trying two?"

Everyone laughed.

Tess made a face.

"You're a literary genius, a bloody brilliant businesswoman, and an all-around superhuman superstar. You can't be gifted at everything, Butterfly," Omar said. "Tell them the rest of the story."

"I picked up Omar and we drove to the harbor."

"She didn't even get out of the car," Omar said with a squeal.

"Well, it was a convertible and he was outside, so there was no need, really. Anyway, I said, 'Thanks, it's been fun, but my friend and I have decided to go to Monaco.' We drove off and spent a fabulous week sunning ourselves."

"Butterfly, you skipped the best part. After she said goodbye to Theo, whose mouth is probably still hanging open to this day, she turned the music up before speeding off. What song happened to be playing? 'Little Red Corvette.' It was just too bloody perfect. I still can't listen to Prince without thinking of that poor famous man on his giant bloody boat."

They all dissolved into hysterics.

Jack leaned closer to Tess. "You were quite the heartbreaker."

"Don't worry, he consoled himself with a bevy of young models, or so the tabloids claimed the following week. Jack, you are the most handsome man I've ever seen. I can only imagine how many girls' dreams you've dashed over the years. I don't know how anyone could possibly spend a moment with you and ever let you go."

He leaned forward and kissed her.

"So Butterfly, shall we tell them more fun stories about your suitors? Perhaps Jack would like to hear about the athletes you dated in your twenties."

"Oh my God, you're going to ruin sports for me," Jack said.

"Only football and baseball," Omar said.

"Clay, kiss your man so he'll shut up," Tess said.

"With pleasure, doubly so," Clay said.

They all laughed.

**

The next morning when Tess woke up, Jack was sitting on the bed holding a white orchid. "Happy Valentine's Day, sweetheart."

"Oh honey, it's so beautiful. Happy Valentine's Day," she replied. "I know it's Omar and Clay's big day, but before we play host and hostess, I need some alone time with you. Stay right there." She dashed off to the bathroom and returned a few minutes later in high heels, a red, lace bra and underwear set, and a matching garter belt.

"Wow!" Jack said, his eyes popping out of his head.

"I didn't know what to get you, so I hope this will do."

He put his hands on her hips and pulled her to him. "Best present ever."

After Jack was finished unwrapping his gift, they cleaned up and went to serve their guests breakfast. They all spent the day lounging on Tess and Jack's private beach. Mid-afternoon, the staff arrived to set up for the wedding, and everyone went to shower and dress. Tess emerged from the bathroom in a long, flowing, yellow sundress with a flower in her hair.

"You are stunning," Jack said, embracing her.

"And you are the sexiest man I have ever seen." She kissed him and said, "I'm going to check on Omar."

She knocked on the door of the guest suite that served as Omar's pre-wedding dressing room.

"Come in," he called. "Oh Butterfly, you look beautiful."

"And you're as handsome as can be," she said, hugging him. "Are you nervous?"

"Not at all. I feel completely at peace."

"I'm so happy for you," she said. "But I wonder if you felt at my wedding a bit of what I'm feeling at yours."

"That it's not just us anymore? Yeah, I felt it too," he said.

"I know Clay is the love of your life, and I love him too, but you and I, we'll always be soul mates."

Omar smiled brightly and hugged her. "Always," he whispered.

Tess sniffled and wiped the corners of her eyes. "Now, let's go get you married."

As the guests walked down to the beach, each was handed a white lei made of orchids. A photographer captured everything. They had a beautiful, simple ceremony on the sand with a justice of the peace, each reciting vows they had written. Clay went first, and then it was Omar's turn.

"I'm sure many people think of me as carefree and fun-loving. Those who know me best understand there is another side. Losing my family at such a young age simply because of who I am, because of who I love, caused me to carry something dark deep within my heart. In some ways, it made me afraid to love. Clay, you changed all that. Loving you and being loved by you, day in and day out, through the good and difficult times, has helped heal what was broken, lightened my spirit, and filled my heart. You've shown me what commitment means, what family can be. I love you now and always."

Tess cried and Jack rubbed her back. When Omar and Clay kissed, there was a rousing round of applause. After hugs and handshakes, the guests sat at a gorgeous table on the beach that overflowed with candles and flowers, beneath a canopy of twinkly lights. At each place setting, there was a heart-shaped keychain and pocketknife engraved with Omar and Clay's names and the date.

Waiters passed around champagne and sparkling water for the toast. Tess stood, raised her glass, and said, "Omar and Clay, I love you both beyond measure. Omar, you've been my family for as long as I care to remember. I know how you searched for true, unconditional love, and I'm so glad you found it with such a wonderful man. Clay, when you and Omar fell in love, you became my family too, and my life is much richer for it. I'm so happy to witness the two of you make your own family official. May you always look at each other with the same adoration and devotion I see in your eyes today, and may your love deepen with each passing year. We all wish you a lifetime of health, happiness, and dreams fulfilled in the safety and love of the home you create together."

"Cheers!" they all said.

"Thank you, Tess," Clay said.

"Yes, thank you, Butterfly," Omar said, wiping tears from his eyes.

Tess sniffled. "Well, enough of that. Let's get to the part Omar really cared about."

"The booze!" Omar jested.

"The feast," Tess said. She signaled to the waitstaff and they served fruity cocktails and a traditional Hawaiian feast, including kalua pork, huli huli chicken, grilled fish, sweet potatoes, poke, and mountains of fresh fruit. After they ate, the entertainment began. They were treated to live Hawaiian music, a hula dancing performance and lesson, and as Omar requested, professional fire eating. After the fire performance, Tess disappeared and came back wearing a grass skirt and bikini top. Omar jumped out of his seat and started clapping and screaming. "This is for you," she said to him, before dancing a choreographed routine with the hula troupe that ended with Tess belly dancing. Everyone loved it. Omar couldn't stop laughing and Jack was transfixed. When they all plopped back down at the table for wedding cake, Tess said to Omar, "Oh, the things I do for you." They enjoyed a spectacular fireworks show over the ocean as they finished their cake. The happy couple and their friends stayed on the beach for hours, drinking, talking, and laughing.

***

The next day, everyone enjoyed brunch on the outdoor veranda. When it was nearly noon, Omar and Clay finally arrived.

"Nice of you to join us," Tess said.

"Point me to the coffee," Omar said. "I didn't get much sleep."

Tess offered an exaggerated wink. "Well, I'm glad things are off to a good start and Clay hasn't had second thoughts yet. You know, Clay, there's still time to get it annulled or plead temporary insanity or something," Tess joked.

"No, so far it's wedded bliss. But you know Omar, he'll start pushing his luck sooner or later," Clay said.

"Ooh, good one. You're catching on with how to deal with him," Tess said.

"Butterfly, perhaps you should don that grass skirt again. I think we'd all love an encore," Omar said, taking a seat with his coffee.

Tess giggled.

Jack leaned over and whispered, "Yeah, I wouldn't mind seeing that again. Maybe a private showing?"

"Don't worry, baby. I saved the skirt," she said, kissing him.

"I must say that the fire eater's body was unbelievable. How do you suppose one gets biceps like that?" Omar asked.

"Thinking of other men already?" Clay asked.

"No, he scared me a little. I mean, can you imagine what an argument with him would be like? A bit too intense for my sensibilities."

They all laughed.

"Now that the guests of honor have graced us with their blissed-out, newlywed presence, I think a toast is in order," Tess said. She turned to Jack. "Will you do the honors?"

Jack raised his glass. "I think I'll keep it simple, like my wife prefers. To family."

"To family!" they all said.

CHAPTER 13

The next morning, Bobby, Gina, Joe, and Luciana thanked their hosts profusely for an unforgettable experience and then flew back to DC on Tess's jet. Omar and Clay spent the next two weeks enjoying their luxurious honeymoon at the Four Seasons, meeting up with Tess and Jack several times. They spent the last day of their vacation at Tess and Jack's house.

The foursome lounged on the beach under umbrellas, and Omar said, "Butterfly, do you want to take a walk?"

"Sure," she said, rising. She slipped on her oversized straw hat and took Omar's hand. They walked along the ocean's edge, letting the warm water splash across their feet.

"You look so relaxed," Tess said.

"Well, I've had two weeks of nonstop sex, days spent lying on the beach, and a steady flow of rum cocktails; who would have guessed that it's a relaxing way to live?" Omar said with a smile. "Oh, and the ninety-minute massage I had yesterday wasn't too shabby either. Don't tell Clay, but wow, my masseur was quite the bit of man candy. If I weren't married, I tell ya."

Tess giggled. "Was the wedding and honeymoon everything you imagined?"

"More," he replied. "I can never thank you and Jack enough for making everything so wonderful."

"There's no need. We're so thrilled for you and Clay. When I see the two of you together, I could burst with joy."

"That's because you know how alone I felt for so many years. Only people like us could really understand," he said. "Of course we've always had each other, which has been a lifeline in every way, but having someone to grow old with, someone to wake up with every day, it's immeasurably special. I've had a lot of happiness in my life, sometimes more than you, ironically because I've so enjoyed your spectacular life. But happiness and contentment aren't the same. Dare I say, I truly feel at peace now."

Tess squeezed his hand.

"I knew you would understand," he said.

"I was telling Jack the same thing recently. When you've had to take care of yourself for ages, you don't take it for granted when you find someone you can count on to always be there. I think that's why the connection is so strong between me and Jack. People don't understand why we're always so affectionate, but from the first night we met, we both knew the other had gone without a certain kind of love, that we had each survived unspeakable pain and loss. From the very beginning, we made an unspoken decision to just love each other with everything we have."

"You make it look easy."

"It is easy," she replied.

"Watching the two of you these past few years is what really pushed me to make my commitment to Clay official. I've seen the change in your eyes, and I guess I wanted to experience it too."

"I'm so glad you have it," she said, smiling.

"You know, I was thinking about how you said our senior year Christmas together was your favorite holiday until you met Jack. Perhaps it was more sacred than I realized, that toxic, all-American meal of ours notwithstanding."

She smiled.

"Promise me something, Butterfly."

"Anything."

"Promise me we will always have this," he said, holding her hand in his and giving it a squeeze. "We will always have us, together with others and quiet moments alone."

She stopped, hugged him tightly, and whispered, "Of course. Now you promise me the same."

"I promise," he whispered, squeezing her tighter.

When they parted, she said, "Are you ready to get back to our gorgeous men?"

"Well, I do love watching how they glisten in the sun. When they come out of the ocean all wet, holy hell."

They both laughed.

"But I think I could use a little more time alone with you, Butterfly."

She smiled. "Me too."

***

As the sun set, they all sat on the veranda for a special farewell dinner prepared and served by a renowned local chef.

"I think our last meal deserves a toast," Jack said.

"If you don't mind, I'd like to make it," Omar said, raising his glass. "To Tess and Jack for giving us the celebration of a lifetime. We love you more than we can possibly say."

"Yes, thank you so much. It's been spectacular," Clay added.

"Cheers," they all said.

"I would also like to say a few words," Tess said.

"The floor is yours, Butterfly."

"Omar and I would like to offer a toast to Clay and Jack. We know that when you fall in love with someone, it isn't always a package deal. Thank you for sharing us. Omar and I love each other so much and we can't tell you how grateful we are that we've never had to choose, that you've both simply accepted our bond."

Everyone smiled and sipped their drinks.

"Tess, I knew from the moment I met Omar that he was a two-for-one deal," Clay said.

"You've always been incredibly generous. I know there are things you've given up so that Omar could travel with me and be there for me," Tess replied.

"It's been my pleasure. Having you in my life has been such a gift. I truly feel doubly blessed," Clay replied.

"I feel the same way about you and Omar, fortunate to have you in my life," Jack said. He turned to Tess and said, "Sweetheart, your friendship with Omar is beautiful. Just being around you two makes me happy."

"Are you guys really going to stay here for another two months? I mean, who could blame you? It's been so blissful that I can hardly stand to go back myself, so I can't imagine why you two ever would with the freedom you have. But I'll miss you so, Butterfly," Omar said.

"I'll miss you too, but we'll be back before Easter, and then we'll be in DC for the whole summer and fall, minus a little time for traveling. Enjoying the salty air is just too good to give up. It's been wonderful for my writing. My new novel is really taking shape."

"Are you ready to tell me what your latest masterpiece is about?" Omar asked.

"Family," Tess replied. "That's all I'm saying for now."

Omar shook his head with a smile.

"What?" Tess asked.

"It's just that you only write about what you know. I'm glad you're finally able to tackle that subject."

Tess smiled. "Well, enough of this seriousness. Let's eat. Oh, and Omar, do tell Clay and Jack about your masseur. I hate to make waves with newlyweds, but since you've spilled so many of my secrets, perhaps you'd like to tell them about your man candy."

"That was cold, Butterfly," Omar said, laughing.

CHAPTER 14

In a flash, Easter weekend was upon them. Jack, Tess, Omar, and Clay pulled up in front of the Miller house, and Mikey and his family followed in the car behind. They all started spilling out of their vehicles and grabbing luggage when Mary and John flung the door open to greet them. The boys ran up the walkway, hugged their grandparents, and flew inside. Mikey and Julie followed.

"How was the trip?" Mary asked, hugging Mikey.

"The kids will never be the same," Mikey said. "Tess's jet was amazing."

"Forget the kids, I don't know how I'll ever fly commercial economy again," Julie said with a laugh. "And we could talk to Clay forever. We have so much in common since we all work in healthcare."

"Hi, Jack," Mary said, embracing him.

"We're glad you're here, son," John said, hugging him.

Tess followed, hugging her in-laws. "Mary, John, this is Omar and his husband Clay."

"Great to meet you both." John extended his hand. "Welcome."

"We're so glad you could join us for the holiday," Mary said.

"It's very kind of you to have us," Omar said.

"You have a lovely home," Clay added, handing her a bag with two bottles of wine and a bouquet of pastel-colored flowers.

"Oh, how sweet. Thank you," Mary said. "John, why don't you show everyone up to their rooms?"

Tess stayed behind as the others trudged upstairs.

"Mary, I wanted to thank you for inviting Omar and Clay. It's so thoughtful and I can't tell you how much it means to me," Tess said.

"Jack said they're your family, so that makes them a part of this family too. We're delighted to have them," Mary said.

Tess unzipped her handbag and took out a large envelope. "These are the photographs you asked for," she said, handing it to Mary.

Mary pulled the photos out. Her eyes became misty. "Oh, you were such a stunning bride. My Jack is so handsome. You both look so happy."

"It was the happiest day of my life," Tess said. "But Jack has made each one since even better."

Mary flipped to the next photo and the tears fell uncontrollably from her eyes. "Gracie is beautiful," she whimpered. "She has my eyes, just like Jack. I see so much of him in her face."

Tess wrapped Mary in a warm hug. "I'd better go upstairs and help Jack unpack."

"Don't be long, dear. I made my famous cobbler," Mary said, sniffling. "We can all have a cup of coffee and get to know each other."

Tess smiled. "We'll be down soon."

"Hey, sweetheart," Jack said when she entered the room. "I put your hanging clothes in the closet."

She slipped her hands around his waist. "Kiss me."

He took her face in his hands and kissed her tenderly.

"Strange how coming here just a few months ago was so different," she said.

"This time, I feel like I belong. That's because of you."

She smiled. "No, it's because you let them see the man you really are."

"You were so hurt last time we were here. I look at the bed and the bathroom just a few feet away and I remember how much pain you were in taking those steps. Does being back here remind you of it?"

"No, baby. It reminds me of you taking care of me, how gentle you were, and how I fell more in love with you every second, which I didn't even think was possible."

"You always see the good," he said, letting out a huff.

She shook her head. "I see it all. I just focus on the bit that matters."

He kissed her again, reluctant to let her go.

"We'd better get downstairs. Your mother made cobbler," she said, turning to walk away.

He grabbed her hand and she turned to face him. They just stared at each other, no words spoken.

***

"Mary, the cobbler was divine," Omar said, scraping up the last bit. "I'm having to restrain myself from licking the plate."

"I'm so glad you enjoyed it," Mary replied. "Tess and I had fun baking together the last time they visited."

"Yes, she's become quite the little baker since hanging out with the president. Butterfly, perhaps we should start calling you the high priestess of pastry."

Tess giggled.

"If you decide to give up on this starving artist thing, maybe you could open a patisserie," he joked.

"That reminds me, Tess, everyone is so excited about your reading at the library on Monday. We put an ad in the newspaper and something on that Facebook," Mary said.

"I'm looking forward to it," Tess replied.

"So, today the boys will color Easter eggs, then we made a reservation for dinner like you and Jack requested, so thoughtful of you. Tomorrow morning is church for whoever wants to go, followed by Easter dinner. Tess, I tried out a few new recipes for some vegetarian dishes," Mary said.

"That's so considerate. Thank you."

"Well, we should clean up these dishes and get to the Easter eggs; I know the boys are eager. Whoever wants to help can join us in the kitchen."

Tess stood up.

"Are you going to color eggs, baby?" Jack asked.

"Yeah, I've never done it before," she said, following Mary.

Omar laughed.

"What's so funny?" Jack asked.

"For a woman who has truly been everywhere and done everything, a woman who has done things most people wouldn't even know to dream of, it always makes me smile when she discovers a new simple pleasure that most people take for granted. I'm pretty sure she's never carved a pumpkin, either."

"Jack, are you coming?" Tess hollered from the kitchen.

"On my way, sweetheart."

***

They arrived at the restaurant and the host escorted them to a private room in the back.

"Thank you," Jack said quietly to his mother.

"Of course, honey," she replied. "It was so nice that you and Tess wanted to take everyone out."

"Our pleasure," he replied.

They had a delicious dinner with nonstop conversation, and afterward, Mary and John took the boys home so the others could stop by the old bar by the barn.

The bar was packed with wall-to-wall people. Mikey noticed a group leaving a booth in the corner and he ran to snag it. Jack and Clay headed to the bar to get the first round for the group. When they returned to the table, Julie was laughing hysterically. "Oh my God, Tess and Omar are so funny," she said.

"I'm glad someone finds him amusing," Tess said with a laugh.

"Butterfly, if we were at Shelby's, I'd be lobbing pretzels at you."

Tess crinkled her nose.

"How did you two meet?" Julie asked.

"Orientation day, our freshman year of college. A bunch of kids ended up on the football field at the end of the evening. Tess and I didn't know each other, but we were both trying to escape the potheads and find some peace. We ended up lying in the grass, staring at the stars, and sharing our deepest hopes and fears." He looked at Tess and they smiled at one another. "Of course I didn't know we'd be stuck together for life."

"It certainly has been tiresome," Tess said.

"Indeed," Omar said, raising his beer bottle. He paused and said, "What the hell are we listening to?"

"Seems like someone in the bar had a hankering for '80s hair metal," Tess said. "My money is on that guy, over there," she said, gesturing to a man sporting a Bon Jovi T-shirt.

"You Americans have the worst taste in music. Add this poor excuse for beer, and bloody hell," Omar said.

"Come on, let's see if you can do any better. There's a jukebox and I'm itching to dance," Tess replied. "Let's get something good in the queue."

"You stay here; Clay and I will go," Omar said.

"Oh no, you're not picking," Tess said.

"Why not?" Omar asked.

"Because I'm not in the mood for Ricky Martin."

"That was cold, Tess. Besides, he's fabulous," Omar said, taking a swig of his beer and heading for the jukebox.

"Clay, we're all counting on you. You have good taste. Control your man," Tess said.

"I'll do my best," Clay said.

"Sara can't wait to see everyone tomorrow. She was so bummed she couldn't come out with us tonight, but it's tough with a newborn. Her in-laws are watching the baby on Monday so she can come to your reading. We should FaceTime her to say hi," Julie said.

"I left my phone in the car," Mikey said.

"Here, use mine," Tess said, sliding her phone across the table.

Jack put his arm around Tess. "Kiss me," he whispered in her ear. She smiled and kissed him softly.

"I love you," he said.

"I love you too, baby."

Just as they finished their call with Sara, Omar and Clay returned.

"Sorry, Tess. I did my best but he's in rare form tonight. We'll be working our way through eighties one-hit wonders," Clay said.

"If 'Say You, Say Me' comes on, I'm going to thrash you," Tess said to Omar.

He laughed. "I considered it, just to get a rise out of you, but don't worry. You'll be happy, Butterfly. After a few songs to make you laugh, I picked two I know you'll love."

Tess smirked.

"Does Jack know about your special tavern talent?" Omar asked.

She shook her head and buried her face in her hands. "What have you done?"

"Don't worry. I threw you a softball. You'll know when it comes on. Besides, it's an American bar loaded with men. Hardly a challenge. Where did we first discover this very special talent of yours? Was it somewhere in Africa?" Omar asked.

"No, it was in Tokyo, in that little karaoke bar we stumbled into in the middle of the night."

Omar smiled. "I know. I just wanted to make you say it."

"You're terrible, and I'm not doing it."

"Yes, you are. I challenge you, and I know you can't help yourself."

"I hate you," Tess said.

"I love you too, Butterfly."

"What are you talking about?" Jack asked. "I know it must be good."

"Oh, it is," Omar said. "Shall I tell them, or would you like the honors?"

"It's all you," Tess said.

"Well, Tess and I spent years trotting around the globe. We were always in a different country, with different people, and we rarely spoke the language. But one constant we noticed was that anywhere you go on this planet, there are bars playing American music, always the same songs. One night in Tokyo, we were saying how much fun it would be to hear people all over the world singing the same songs together. The next thing I knew, our sweet and ridiculously charismatic Tess had everyone in the bar singing at the top of their lungs. It became a thing: everywhere we went; Tess would get everyone in bars, pubs, clubs, whatever, to sing. I've seen it a thousand times and I still don't quite know how she manages it, but it's splendid. We slept in hotels every night for weeks, months, years on end. Nothing was ever the same, so this became our constant."

Tess smiled. "Yeah, this and poached eggs."

"Right you are," Omar said with a smile. "We'll always have poached eggs. But nothing can beat the singing."

"Yeah, and it was a good reminder," Tess said.

"Of what, sweetheart?" Jack asked.

"Of the common humanity people share when you look beyond the details."

Jack smiled.

Tess turned to Omar. "I'm not doing it."

"Yes, you are," Omar said, winking.

Just then, "Major Tom" came on. "You did not," Tess said.

"Go on, Butterfly, get your groove on. There are a few more songs and then our challenge begins."

Tess jumped up. "Come on Clay and Julie, it's all us." The three made their way to the center of the bar and started dancing.

Omar laughed. "Watch her when he sings, 'Four, three, two, one.' Tess throws her arms up and goes nuts. It's so funny. I'm surprised no one's put it on YouTube yet."

Tess, Clay, and Julie danced to a slew of songs, all the best of the eighties. Jack couldn't take his eyes off Tess. Then "Don't Stop Believin'" came on, and Tess pointed at Omar and started laughing. He raised his beer bottle and nodded gallantly. "Here we go," he said to Jack and Mikey. They watched as Tess tapped a guy on the shoulder and said something to him. He smiled and said something to his friends. They all turned toward Tess and started singing, waving their arms up to direct others. People began catching on, and by the time the first pre-chorus hit, everyone in the bar was belting it out. Tess stood in the center of the joyful pandemonium, singing and laughing. Omar held his beer bottle up and she winked at him in return. Mikey was laughing hysterically. Jack was mesmerized.

"We've heard people in countless cities in more than fifty countries singing this song with every accent you can imagine. It's hard to explain how magical it was. As she hears these people singing it tonight, she hears echoes of them all. Tess was often so melancholy on the road, but this always made her happy. I'm so glad she's finally enjoying her extraordinary life," Omar said. He and Jack clinked beer bottles. Jack looked back at Tess, unable to stop smiling.

Halfway through the song, Jack noticed Tess's phone ringing. He said, "Mick's trying to video call Tess."

"Leave her be. I'll get it," Omar said. He swiped to answer the call. "Hey, Mick. Can you hear me?"

"Hey, Omar. Barely. Where are you guys?"

"In a bar in Pennsylvania. We're with Jack and his brother. Tess has everyone in the bar singing along to a Journey song."

Mick laughed. "Of course she does. Hi, Jack."

"Hey, Mick," Jack said.

"I can get her for you, but I think you'd rather see this. She doesn't know it, but 'Tiny Dancer' is up next," Omar said.

"Perfect. I was calling for a dose of sunshine. Keep me on the line so I can watch her dance when it comes on."

"Ah, it's about to start. At least you can hear us now. I wonder why she loves this song so bloody much anyway," Omar said.

"No idea," Jack said.

"I know," Mick said. "She never told me, but I know."

"Do tell," Omar said.

"Tess told me you two have always understood each other," Jack said.

"Few people can know what it's like. Only those with an artist's soul who have spent their entire adult life in the fishbowl can understand. I met Tess when she was twenty-three. I knew it was only the beginning of her success. So much talent and so smart. Omar, tell me something: You've known Tess since before the world did. Has she changed?"

Omar shook his head. "Not at all, not in the way you mean."

"Exactly. She hasn't changed a single bit since I met her either. That's a hard trick to pull off in our world, to never lose yourself. The way you manage it is to choose to remain calm like the eye of a storm. Tess does that better than anyone I've ever known because she never gets distracted by the illusion, she never loses sight of what's real. What's real and true is all that matters to her, moment to moment. She loves this song because of six little words, 'Oh, how it feels so real.' Watch her face when that lyric comes."

Jack smiled.

"Ooh, we're almost at the pre-chorus. I'll hold the phone up so you can watch," Omar said.

Just as those lyrics hit, Tess closed her eyes, singing those six words as if she were the only one who heard them, an enormous smile across her face. Jack watched as she twirled in the center of the room, a bar full of people singing around her.

***

On Easter Sunday, they all went to church. Soon after they arrived back at the house, Sara and Bill arrived with their new daughter. After greetings and introductions, Mary started heating up the food she had been preparing for days. John sat in his recliner, cooing at his baby granddaughter. The others went outside for a game of touch football. Still recovering from childbirth, Sara stood on the sidelines, heckling and cheering. During one play, Jack tried to get past Tess and she tackled him, both of them tumbling to the ground, laughing.

"Hey, it's supposed to be touch football," Jack said, pulling her on top of him.

"Yeah, but if I played by those rules, we wouldn't be like this right now," she said, leaning down to kiss him.

"Okay, you two lovebirds, pay attention. Butterfly, if our team beats Jack and Mikey, I'll feel good about myself for eons," Omar said.

Tess craned her neck to look at him. "That's hardly an incentive to do my best. I suspect that a win will make you even more insufferable," she said, giggling.

"You two are hysterical," Sara said.

"Oh, just wait until there are cocktails. That's when I'm at peak hilarity," Omar said.

"Hey," Jack said softly. "Kiss me again."

"Don't have to ask me twice." She pressed her lips gently to his, settling onto his body.

"Happy Easter, baby," he said.

"Happy Easter."

***

"Everything looks great, Mom," Jack said as they all sat down at the table.

"Before we dig into this feast, I would like to say how happy Mary and I are to have you all here. It's hard to understand until you get to be our age, but when you look back on your life, what you care about are the people who matter the most to you. That's what I see when I look around this table. We're so grateful to have our three children here with the beautiful, loving families they have created. I know many of us here come from different religious backgrounds, but I'm sure we all feel thanks on this day. With that said, we thank the Lord for this bounty and all the blessings bestowed upon this family. Amen."

"Amen," everyone said.

"Please help yourselves," Mary said. "John, would you serve the ham?"

They all began eating.

"This is wonderful," Clay said.

Mary smiled.

"John, what you said was very nice. Tess is probably the least religious person at this table, although she's probably the only one who has been exposed to just about every religion on this planet, not to mention all the religious icons she's met. Butterfly, I've always thought that you're secretly the most spiritual person I know," Omar said.

"I don't know about that," Tess replied.

"I do," Omar said.

"Who have you met?" Jack asked.

"Who she hasn't met would be a shorter list," Omar said, taking a forkful of mashed potatoes.

"I met the Dalai Lama. Lovely man," Tess said. She turned toward Omar and said, "Too bad you weren't on that trip. You would have enjoyed him so much. He was very thoughtful, deeply kind. He's completely present in the moment, as I aspire to be. I felt at peace around him."

"I'm just grateful I was with you when you met the pope. That was surreal." Omar turned his attention to the group. "The driver took us underground, directly into the Vatican to a top-secret spot. We saw things that are definitely *not* on the standard tour."

"Wow," John said.

"The antiques in that place would blow your mind," Omar said.

"You met the pope?" Mary asked, her eyes wide.

"Oh, don't get too excited, I doubt Tess will be invited back," Omar said with a chuckle.

Tess rolled her eyes.

"Come on, Butterfly. Most people are awestruck to meet the pope. You gave him a lecture."

"I did no such thing. We simply had an honest little chat about women's autonomy and freedom."

"Yes, go Tess!" Sara said, holding her hand up for a high-five.

"Really, he's a nice man, we just don't agree on very much," Tess said.

Everyone sat, their mouths agape.

"He certainly appreciated what you do. He told Tess that he's aware that her books help people around the world, and he commended her for how charitable she is," Omar said.

Tess shrugged. "It's easy to feel lost. Life is challenging. People need different things to get through it, to make sense of it and figure out where they fit. For some it's religion, for others it could be meditation, exercise, travel, art, music, or even novels. I understand that, which is why I've always attended every service and ceremony I've been invited to, even though I rarely share the beliefs."

"So Butterfly, you've seen more of this world than most can dream of. In your travels, you've been exposed to many variants of Hinduism, Buddhism, Islam, Judaism, Christianity, Taoism, Shinto, and goodness, so many more. You've sat beside those practicing and worshipping across the globe and have had conversations with their leaders. Did any of it resonate?"

"I'm sure I picked up bits and pieces, mostly about the searching people do and the human desire for connection, belonging, and meaning." She smiled. "There was one thing, actually. As you know, I would never follow any organized religion. I find them exclusionary by design. However, I learned about the Baha'i faith when I was in Tehran. It's fascinating because this now-global faith originated in Iran, but those who practice it there do so under great persecution. Anyway, Baha'i teaches that there is a oneness in all world religions. By extension, there is a oneness of humanity. *That* idea holds power to me."

"That's beautiful," Jack said.

"There's a gorgeous Baha'i temple I visited in Uganda. If we ever make it to Africa together one day, perhaps we can go."

"I would love that," he replied, stroking her cheek.

Returning her attention to the table, she said, "The Baha'i faith actually adopts the teachings of many religions. It's sort of like a blended family. We all bring our histories with us, and they must be respected and valued; when we come together, we become something else, something greater, and we connect through our shared humanity. We tap into our oneness."

Everyone smiled.

"Tess, you're my hero. Did you really scold the pope?" Sara asked.

"Oh yeah, we won't be going back to Rome," Omar said. "But fear not, we'll always be welcome at Mick's London pad, and I hear you'd love to meet him."

They all laughed.

As the conversation moved on, Jack leaned over and kissed Tess on the cheek.

"What's that for, baby?" she whispered.

"For bringing oneness to my life," he whispered. "I love you so much. Thank you for being my family."

She combed her fingers through his hair. "Forever and always, my love. Nothing could ever come between us."

EPILOGUE

The Next Day

Mary drove Jack and Tess to the library an hour before the scheduled reading, and discovered that the streets were lined with cars a mile in every direction. When they arrived at the library, they were stunned to see a mob waiting outside and several police cars coordinating crowd control.

"Thank goodness I can park in one of the reserved spots," Mary said. "You two wait here while I see what's going on."

When Mary returned to the car, she said, "It seems that thousands of people have shown up for your reading, dear. They've come from all over. The police won't allow everyone in because we've far exceeded capacity. They say it's already standing room only. Thankfully, I had them put signs on the chairs in the first two rows, reserving them for our family and the Pattersons."

They all got out of the car. Jack took Tess's hand and they walked slowly through the crowd to the main entrance. People were taking pictures of Tess on their cell phones as she smiled and said "hello" and "thank you for coming." Many were holding copies of her books, and she promised to come outside and sign them after her reading. Mary rushed Tess through the crowd inside to a back room where she could wait. On the way, she noticed people with piles of her books on their laps, some with overflowing tote bags. Jack waited with Tess until fifteen minutes before the reading, and then left to join his family in the audience.

After he left, Tess cracked the door open to sneak a look at the audience. Jack, the Miller clan, Omar, and Clay were seated in the front row. The Pattersons, including Genevieve, were seated behind them. She returned to the back room and texted Omar: *Please come see me.*

"Butterfly beckons. I'll be back in a flash," he said to Clay and Jack.

A few minutes later, Omar rushed over to Jack. "I need to speak with you privately."

Jack followed him to a quiet corner in the back of the library near Tess's waiting spot. "What's up?"

"Slight hiccup. Tess is nervous. Nervous is an understatement, really. She's completely freaking out."

"Seriously? Tess never gets nervous."

"I know. She's spoken in front of presidents, prime ministers, and rock stars; she's been in arenas all over the world in front of thousands, and done countless talks guarded by men holding machine guns, not to mention a slew of high-profile television appearances. The one thing my Butterfly has never gotten is butterflies. Suddenly, at this modest library in the middle of Pennsylvania, she's practically hyperventilating. Everything I say seems to make it worse."

"What did you say?" Jack asked.

"Well, a pep talk is new territory for us, so I tried reminding her that she's Tess Fucking Lee. She said, 'Oh my God,' and started pacing in a circle. Then, I tried reminding her she's Tess Miller. She threw me out of the room. In all the years we've known each other, I've never seen her nervous."

"I have, once: the day we announced that we were getting married. She cared so much about what you would think and was a wreck. This is because we're all here."

Omar smiled. "Of course. Can you help? If she hasn't escaped through the window, she's in there," he said, pointing to the back room.

"I'm on it. Go sit with everyone," Jack said.

Omar nodded.

Jack knocked on the door.

"Yeah," Tess muttered.

He opened the door and found Tess leaning against the wall, her head between her knees, trying to catch her breath. He walked over and rubbed her back. "Sweetheart, what's wrong?"

"I think I'm having a panic attack. I'm not really sure because I don't know what they feel like, but I sort of think it must feel like this."

"Calm down. Deep breaths," he said. "It's okay."

She raised her head and looked at him. "I feel like I'm going to pass out and my heart is racing."

"You've done a million of these things. What's going on? Talk to me, sweetheart."

"It's just…"

"What, baby?"

"I never had a family there before."

He smiled and put his hand on her face. "Yes you have. You've had Omar and you've had me."

"This is different," she said softly.

"Come here," he said, embracing her. He wrapped his arms tightly around her, encircling her in his protection and love. "They're your family. They love you. There's nothing to worry about. Just stay here in my arms until you're ready."

After a couple of minutes, Tess pulled away.

"Do you feel better?" Jack asked.

She nodded. "You're my rock. You always make me feel better."

"They love you and you can count on it. It's real, sweetheart. Just lean into it. Be you. That's all anyone wants."

"Kiss me, Jack."

He kissed her gently. "I love you with my whole heart, forever."

She took a slow, deep breath. "I love you too. Okay, I'm ready now."

Jack walked Tess to the doorway, where she was asked to wait to be introduced. He kissed her again, smiled, and returned to his seat. He nodded at Omar, letting him know everything was okay.

Mary approached the podium and tapped the microphone to make sure it was working. "This is a very special treat for our community and for my family. Tess Lee is one of the most celebrated authors in the world. Her novels have inspired hundreds of millions of people, showing them that there is a path through their pain, light on the other side, and infinite possibilities for love, hope, and redemption. I couldn't be more excited to introduce one of America's most prolific, honored, and beloved authors, and a woman I personally love very much, my daughter-in-law, Tess Lee."

Tess emerged to a massive standing ovation, her family in the front row. She placed her silver pen on the podium, with the words

Tess Miller oriented to face her. She smiled at Jack and began, reading selections from fan favorites, *Candy Floss, Blue Moon,* and *Ray of Light.*

"Before we get to the book signing, I wanted to do something I've never done before. I hope you'll indulge me as I read an excerpt from the unpublished novel I'm currently working on."

Everyone clapped vigorously.

"It's called *Holiday Homes,* and it's about family, something I've been thinking about a lot lately. Really, it explores loss, missed opportunities, and the human need for connection that we all share. I started writing it when I was here last, and it's dedicated to my family seated right there in the front row," she said gesturing and smiling. Jack smiled at her and she began reading.

> "She walked down the no-name street in a no-name town in small town America, wondering where she belonged. As the cold December air hit her face, she looked at each house, imagining the different kinds of families, each warm and toasty inside. Suddenly, a scream. She turned to see a little girl, headlights upon her. Racing over, she shoved the girl to safety. In the flash of light, she saw the face of the daughter that couldn't be saved; someone else's daughter would have to do, a different family to remain whole. After the car slammed into her body, she lay on the cold concrete, the noise around her fading, a feeling of peacefulness washing through her. It's a clear night, she thought, staring at the dark sky lit up with stars. I hope the little girl is okay, the little girl saved from the headlights, and the other one who could not be saved, still shining brightly like a star that died long before its light reached us.
>
> "She saw Orion, the hunter. Is the hunter seeking something she doesn't yet have, or is she seeking something already within, she wondered.

When the hunter finds what she longs for, will she return home? What treasures will she bring the others from her travels? As she lay on the frozen ground, she decided that Orion was her favorite constellation. She laughed, thinking about how everything is connected after all. There are no accidents. Constellations are like families, just random groups of stars, near each other by chance, but they recall something familiar to us, so we see a pattern in the randomness. The universe was made up of stars and people who found themselves clumped together by chance, because someone walked into a bar one night, wandered onto a football field one day, birthed a child one morning, or fell in love with someone in an instant. And yet, there's something so familiar, so clear it feels like it couldn't be any other way. And so, we cling to the connections.

"She heard voices telling her, 'Stay with us.' She tried to tune out the noise. There were still questions to answer. Why do we look at the stars? Is it to imagine other worlds or to connect us to our own, like the very stardust of which we are made? Where do I belong? If I return to stardust, will I be a part of a constellation? Will he look up in the night sky and see me, a pattern in the randomness? The voices became louder. 'Stay with us,' they beckoned. Okay, she thought. My stardust shall remain here for now, with him, with them, with the imperfectly perfect, impossibly possible family of which I'm a part, by choice or by glorious happenstance."

SUGGESTED CLASSROOM OR BOOK CLUB USE

1. What do you think about Tess and Jack's relationship? What is special about their relationship, and why is their bond so strong?
2. The friendship between Tess and Omar is the other primary "love" story in this novel. What do you think about their relationship? What does this relationship say about the families we choose? Can you draw comparisons between this friendship and any of your own?
3. *Constellations* explores the nature of family in every sense of the word. What does this novel suggest about the families we are born into and those we create?
4. Tess helps Jack reconnect with his childhood family. How does she do this? What are some examples? What does her love look like in action?
5. Jack cares for Tess when she is injured. How does he do this? What are some examples? What does his love look like in action?
6. How do the characters communicate with each other? Consider the verbal and physical aspects of their communication. What do their patterns of interaction reveal about their relationships?
7. Intimacy is a guiding theme in *Constellations*. What does intimacy look like in this book? What are some examples? What's the purpose of this theme?
8. Grief, loss, and a sense of missed opportunities come up throughout this novel. What are some examples? How do the characters navigate these issues?
9. Tess never shines a spotlight on her good deeds or charitable giving. Why? What can we learn from her about the nature of giving?
10. *Constellations* is a book about love. What is the overall message about love? Find some examples that support your position.

CREATIVE WRITING ACTIVITIES

1. Bobby, Gina, Joe, Luciana, Clay, and each of the Millers are supporting characters. Select one of these characters and write their story.

2. Select one of the characters and look ahead five years. Write a short story based on where you think they end up.

3. If *Constellations* were a play instead of a novel, it would likely include monologues by the main characters. Select a character and write their pivotal monologue.

4. In the final chapter, Tess reads from her latest novel, *Holiday Homes*. Use this scene or imagine a different part of the novel to write an original short story.

5. Write an alternative ending to *Constellations*.

QUALITATIVE RESEARCH ACTIVITIES

1. Select several scenes and perform discourse or conversation analysis on the dialogue. For example, use one of the conversations at Shelby's Bar or the bar by the barn, a conversation between Tess and Jack, a conversation at the Miller house, or any other exchange.

2. Research families and locate peer-reviewed articles or scholarly essays on related issues (e.g., chosen families, LGBTQ+ families, nuclear families). Use your findings to write a paper, using one of the character's experiences to illustrate or challenge your research.

ART ACTIVITIES

1. Create a visual or audiovisual version of the scene that Tess recites from her novel, *Holiday Homes*.

2. Respond artistically to *Constellations*. Using any medium – literary, visual, or performative – create an artistic response to a theme in the novel or express how the novel made you feel.

AUTHOR Q&A

How would you describe Constellations?

It's a love story about family – those into which we're born and those we create. It also explores the human desire to belong and feel connected, missed opportunities and redemption, the true and multilayered nature of intimacy, and the power of love to heal and redeem. This book came to me like a bolt and held my hand. I hope it does the same for others. It's very special to me; it's my personal favorite of my own books, and the epilogue includes my all-time favorite line.

As a follow-up to Shooting Stars *and* Twinkle, *this is the third Tess Lee and Jack Miller novel. What inspired you to keep writing about them?*

I absolutely love these characters, not only Tess and Jack, but all of their friends and loved ones. Of all my books, these characters are nearest and dearest to me. When I finished *Shooting Stars*, I knew there were more stories to tell and I hoped readers would enjoy following their journey as much as I love writing about them. I'm using these characters to explore love, to write a grand love letter to love in all its forms and with all its complexities, one that will unfold over at least five books. If *Constellations* is your introduction to these characters, see how Tess and Jack met, in the first chapter of *Shooting Stars*, reprinted at the end of this book.

What can we expect from the rest of the Tess Lee and Jack Miller novels?

Each novel explores love at the intersection of another topic. Each novel also has its own theme, linked to that exploration. The characters are who they are, so trauma, healing, grief, and loss resurface, as do themes of darkness and light. There are a few things I can promise. Each novel opens with a scene featuring just Tess and Jack; this is, after all, their love story. Each novel concludes with an epilogue, which could be set anywhere from a day to a year later. Each epilogue ends with Tess speaking, because she is our heroine. Tess and Jack will always love each other, although each book contains a dramatic event that will test them. While new characters may appear, the friends you've gotten to know are an important part of all the novels and we learn more about the back stories of these relationships as we progress. Each book also includes an excerpt from one of Tess's novels. I've tried to balance drama with humor in all the novels, so there's a mix of tearful moments and those that make me laugh out loud. In these ways, I hope the books balance darkness and light, mirroring the very story they will ultimately tell. I can also promise that all questions will be answered once you've read all the novels in the series. For example, we learn about Tess's struggle with food in the first novel, *Shooting Stars*, but we don't learn the reasons why until the fourth novel. By following these characters across multiple novels, I'm able to go back further into their stories, drawing out themes and connections.

Can you give any hints about the next Tess Lee and Jack Miller novel?

There's a clue in the last line of the final chapter in *Constellations*, before the epilogue. I will say this: Tess and Jack's relationship will be challenged in a way it never has been before. Readers will also get answers to lingering questions from the earlier novels as loose ends are tied up.

What do you hope readers will take away from Constellations*?*

We can build families of choice. True intimacy is possible when we love unconditionally, whether it comes in the form of sexual passion, the way we laugh with one another, or the way we take care of one another during our darkest or most vulnerable moments. Redemption is possible. If we reflect on missed opportunities, we can try harder and do better. Every relationship matters. Those we've loved are never really gone, even when they are no longer in our lives, and even when they return to stardust.

SHOOTING STARS, CHAPTER 1

"How's your son doing in school?" Tess asked the bartender.

"Really well. He especially loves the history course he's taking."

A man came in and sat two stools down from Tess. They looked at each other and smiled in acknowledgment.

"Hey, Jack. The usual?" the bartender asked.

Jack nodded. "Please."

Tess continued chatting with the bartender as he served Jack a bottle of beer. "The humanities are so important. It's a shame they're undervalued," she said.

"You're the expert," the bartender replied.

Just then, a different man sidled up to Tess. "You have the most beautiful brown eyes," he said.

"Do I?" she asked.

"And the way your hair flows all the way down your back. You know what they say about dirty blondes?"

"I don't think you should finish that sentence," Tess said.

"I've been watching you. Can I buy you a drink?" he asked.

"No, thank you," she replied.

"Come on, just one drink. I'm a nice guy."

"No, thank you," she said, turning away.

The "nice guy" opened his mouth to protest, but Jack stood up with an imposing air and said, "The lady said no."

The man huffed and walked away.

"Thank you," Tess said.

"Don't mention it. I did feel a little sorry for him, though. You are beautiful and I can't blame him for taking a shot."

Tess smiled and pulled out the stool next to her. "Please, scooch over. Let me buy your drink."

He smiled and took the seat next to her. "My name is Tess Lee," she said.

"Jack Miller," he replied. "But it's on me. Yours looks nearly empty. What are you having?"

"Sparkling water. I don't drink. It's just a personal choice," she replied.

"Another sparkling water for my new friend," Jack said to the bartender. "So, Tess, what brings you here by yourself?"

"I was supposed to meet my best friend, Omar, but he had a last-minute emergency. His partner, Clay, was pulled over tonight and it became an incident."

"What was he pulled over for?" Jack asked.

"Being Black," Tess replied. "Clay is a surgeon and was on his way home from the hospital. He was pulled over for no reason and harassed. It's happened to him before. Once, he was on his way to an emergency at the hospital, and he was detained even after he showed his hospital ID. It's egregious. Anyway, I told Omar to stay home with him. They need time together to process and decompress. I was already in a cab on my way here, so I decided to come anyway. I moved to DC from LA about six months ago and I don't have that much of a life yet, I suppose. And you?"

"My friends ditched me. We usually get together on Friday nights at a different bar, but they all had to stay late at work. This place is right down the block from my apartment."

"So, what do you do?" she asked.

"I'm a federal agent with the Bureau, working in counterterrorism. I joined the military right out of high school, Special Forces. I was in the field, often deep undercover, until about a year ago, when I took a desk job as the head of my division."

"Wow, you're like the real-life Jack Bauer. You even look a little like him, with that whole rugged, handsome, hero thing you have going on," she said.

He blushed. "I promise you I'm no Jack Bauer, even on my best day. People thought that character was so tragic, but the real tragedy is that Jack Bauer doesn't exist and you're stuck with guys like me."

She smiled. "What made you choose that line of work?"

"My father was in the military and then became a firefighter. The idea of service always seemed important. I wanted to serve my country, to protect people. It's hard to explain, but when I see someone innocent being threatened, I'm willing to do whatever is necessary to protect them. I know it sounds cliché, but I feel like it's my purpose in life."

"That's noble," she said.

He shook his head. "The lived reality often isn't. When you spend most of your life in the abyss, it gets pretty dark."

"A residue remains, right?" she asked.

He looked at her intently, a little surprised. "Yes, exactly."

"I understand. You convince yourself it's all been for something that matters more than you do, that whatever part of yourself you sacrificed was worth it, because it simply has to be."

He looked at her as if she had read his innermost thoughts. "Yes," he said softly. "Tell me, what do you do?"

"I'm a novelist."

"What are your books about?" he asked.

"That's a hard question to answer. I guess I wanted to write about everything: what it means to live a life, why it's so hard, and how it could be easier. Perhaps my goals were too lofty, and in that respect, each book fails more spectacularly than the one before."

The bartender smirked.

Tess wistfully said, "Maybe reality can never live up to our dreams."

They continued talking, completely engrossed with one another. Two hours later, Jack said, "I live nearby. Do you want to come over for a cup of coffee?"

Tess looked him straight in his warm, blue eyes. "I'd love to."

Jack threw some money down on the bar to cover both tabs. The bartender said, "Ms. Lee, are you sure you're all right? I can call you a cab."

"You're very kind, but I'm fine. Thank you."

Jack opened the door and held it for Tess. "Do you know the bartender?"

"Just met him tonight," she replied.

"Down this way," Jack said, taking her hand as if it were completely natural. They approached a homeless man on the corner asking for money. Tess walked right up to him, pulled a twenty dollar bill from her pocket, and handed it to him. She held his hand as she passed the bill, looked in his eyes, and said, "Be well."

As they walked away, Jack said, "That was really sweet, but you should be more careful."

"I trust my instincts," she replied.

When they arrived at Jack's small apartment, he took her coat. She glanced around and noticed the walls were completely bare. "How long have you lived here?" she asked.

"About nine years," he replied. "Can I get you some coffee or something else to drink?"

She shook her head and meandered over to his bedroom. He followed. He took the back of her head in his hand and started to kiss her, gently and with increasing passion. He pulled off his shirt and they continued kissing. He pulled back to look at her and she noticed the scars on his body: two on his right shoulder, another on his abdomen, and smaller marks along his upper arms. When he noticed her looking, he turned around to lower the light, revealing the gashes across his back. She brushed her fingers along the deep marks. "I'm sorry," he said. "War wounds. A couple of gunshots. Some other stuff from when I was in the Gulf. I know it's gruesome."

"It's wonderful," she whispered.

"What?" he said.

"I'm sorry, I didn't mean it that way. It's just that I've never seen anyone whose outsides match my insides."

He looked at her sympathetically.

"I was abused when I was little. My grandfather and my uncle. It started when I was eight. No one can see my wounds, but they're there."

He stood still, looking at her.

"I'm so sorry. I've never shared that with any man I've been with in my entire life, and I just met you. That has to be the least sexy thing ever. I'll leave," she stammered, trying to walk past him.

He took her hand and pulled her back toward him. He cupped her face in his hands, gently caressed her cheeks, and kissed her. They made love with their eyes locked on to each other. Afterward, he held her in his arms and said, "That was so special. Spend the day with me tomorrow."

"Okay," she replied, and they fell asleep, their limbs entangled.

***

The next morning, Tess awoke to find a note on the pillow beside her that read, "Went to get breakfast. There's an extra toothbrush on the bathroom counter. Back soon."

She brushed her teeth, and by the time she was done, Jack had returned.

"Hey, sweetheart," he said, as if they had known each other for years. He pecked her on the cheek. "I didn't know what you like so I got bagels, muffins, and a fruit salad. Do you want coffee?"

"Yes, please."

He poured two mugs of coffee and they sat down at the small table. "What kind of food do you like, anyway?" he asked.

"I'm a vegetarian. I don't believe in hurting living beings."

Jack looked down.

"Innocent beings," she said.

He smiled. "I guess that's why you're so tiny."

She started picking at the fruit salad. Jack noticed that she was moving it around with her fork, almost like she was counting. He looked at her quizzically.

"I'm weird with food. I don't eat that much. It's kind of a control thing," She paused, keeping her eyes on her breakfast. "I have problems."

He reached across the table and put his hand on hers. "That's okay. We all have problems. They make us human."

They spent the day together, talking, watching TV, and walking around his neighborhood. They got Chinese takeout for dinner and made love twice more. Sunday morning, Tess realized she'd missed a dozen calls and text messages from Omar. She called him while Jack was making coffee.

"I promise, I'm fine. I'm sorry I worried you. I met someone. His name is Jack. He's special... Well, if he is holding me hostage, don't pay the ransom. I want to stay... I'll text you all about it... Okay, love you, too. Bye."

"He was worried about you?" Jack asked.

"He's been looking out for me for a long time. We talk every day, but I guess I was too preoccupied yesterday," she said, slipping her hands around his waist.

"Sounds like a good friend," Jack said.

"He's more than that; he's my family. He moved here a year ago and convinced me to leave LA so we could be in the same city. But enough about him. Right now, I'm only interested in you. Come here," she said, walking backward toward his bedroom. Just as he was about to touch her, she grabbed a pillow and walloped him.

"Oh, you're in trouble now," he said, darting for a pillow. They tumbled onto the bed, laughing.

They spent the rest of the day lounging around Jack's apartment, reading the Sunday newspaper, and sharing stories. That night before they went to sleep, Jack said, "I don't want the weekend to end. Do you have to work tomorrow?"

"Well, I do work for myself. Can you take the day off?"

"I once took two weeks off, but other than that, I've never taken a single day off in over twenty years. So yeah, I think I'm due for a personal day."

***

The next day, Tess and Jack went for a walk and ended up at a local park. They sat on a bench, huddled together in the chilly, late autumn weather. Suddenly, a little boy ran over and tugged at Tess's coat sleeve.

"Do you have superpowers?" he asked. "My dad says you do."

"Excuse me?" she said.

His father came running over. "I'm so sorry if he was bothering you, Ms. Lee."

"Not at all," she replied with a gracious smile.

"I'm a librarian. I want to thank you for everything you've done," he said.

"My pleasure," she replied. "Thank you for what *you* do."

The little boy tugged at her sleeve again. "Well? Do you have superpowers?"

His father laughed. Tess looked at the boy and lowered her voice conspiratorially. "I'll tell you a secret. Everyone has superpowers, they just don't know it."

"Even me?" he asked.

"Especially you," she replied.

Jack smiled.

The man took his son's hand. "I think we've bothered these people enough. Thank you again, Ms. Lee," he said, leading his son down the path.

Jack looked at Tess. "That was so sweet, what you said to that boy."

She leaned over and kissed him.

"What was the deal with his father? It seemed like he knew you."

"I did some volunteer work for the library a few months ago," she replied.

A few little girls came skipping past them, drawing their attention.

"It's starting to get cold. You want to go to a movie?" Jack asked.

"Sure."

After the movie, they went to a neighborhood Italian restaurant for dinner. The maître d' greeted Tess like an old friend. "Ms. Lee, such a pleasure. We have our best table for you."

"I guess you've been here before," Jack said as he pulled out her chair.

"Jack, listen to the music," she said.

"Sinatra – the best."

"Let's dance," she said.

He looked around. "I don't think they have dancing here."

"But I love to dance," she said.

He stood up, took her hands, and they danced by the table. "You know, I'm not much of a dancer, but I promise to dance to as many slow songs as you want."

"Maybe someday we'll have a special song," she said, nuzzling into his chest.

Later, when they got back to Jack's apartment, he led her to the couch with a slightly serious look. "I need to tell you something."

"What is it?" she asked.

"You've seen the scars on my body, but there's another side of it. Tess, I've done things – things that may be unimaginable to someone as sweet as you, things I had to do to protect innocent people." He proceeded to tell her every act of violence he had ever committed, his life laid bare at her feet. The list was long, the death count high.

When he finished, she said, "You did what you had to do for your job. I don't understand why you're telling me this."

"Because I'm in love with you. I'm completely madly in love with you and I've never felt that way about anyone. With the things I've done, I don't expect that you could ever feel that way about me, but I needed you to know who I am." He looked down.

She stroked his cheek. "Jack, I'm in love with you, too. I spent our first night together memorizing your face: every line, edge, ridge, pore. I knew you were the best thing that would ever happen to me and I was afraid the memory would have to last a lifetime."

"I feel like the luckiest man in the world."

"Jack, let's not worry about all of the details of our pasts. I want to leave the pain behind and just love each other now."

He smiled. "Okay, but maybe I should at least know how old you are and when your birthday is."

"Thirty-eight, and I never cared for holidays, including birthdays."

"Got it. Forty-two and you're the only present I'll ever need."

She smiled.

"Let's go to bed," he said.

The next morning, Jack went to work and Tess went home. At the end of the day, they met at his apartment. "I have something for you," he said, holding out a velvet box. "I was passing an antique store and saw it in the window."

She opened the box to reveal a gold heart locket. She beamed and her eyes filled with tears. "Jack, it's the best present I've ever received," she said, putting it around her neck. "I'll wear it every day."

"You have my heart, Tess. My whole heart, forever."

"Promise me something. Don't ever buy me another present again. Nothing could ever be better than this."

"I'm hoping life is long. That's a lot of birthdays, holidays, Tuesdays," he said.

"Flowers. You can always get me flowers if you want to," she replied.

"Which ones are your favorite?"

"White hydrangeas. I never buy them for myself," she said.

They kissed, and then Jack got up and turned some music on. He reached for her hand. "Let's dance."

The second song that played was "All of Me." Two lines into the song, Jack said, "This is our song, I just know it is. Okay, baby?"

She nodded and rested her head on his chest.

They continued to work each day and spend each night together. Thursday night, Tess made eggplant parmesan, which she brought over to share with Jack. While they were eating, he said, "My friends and I go to this place called Shelby's Bar every Friday night. I told them all about you and they really want to meet you. Will you meet us there?"

"Of course," she said. "Tell me about them."

"Joe is in his mid-fifties. We've worked together for about fifteen years. He's a class act. Bobby is young, twenty-nine, and the nicest, most laid-back guy. He joined the Bureau three years ago, but I feel like I've known him forever. His girlfriend, Gina, is an elementary school art teacher. You'll like her."

"Sounds great. What do you think about bringing an overnight bag and staying the night at my place after we hang out with your friends? It's about time you see it. Omar and Clay are coming over for brunch on Saturday and I'm dying for you to meet each other. Will you?"

"Absolutely," he replied.

"Jack, you know how people always talk about all the things they want to do or see in their lifetime? They don't even mention being happy because I suppose they think that's just a given."

"Yeah."

"Happiness has never been a given for me. I guess I pursued other things," she said.

"Me too," he replied.

"But I'm so happy now, with you."

"I love you so much, Tess."

"I love you, too."

ABOUT THE AUTHOR

Patricia Leavy, Ph.D., is an independent scholar and bestselling author. She was formerly Associate Professor of Sociology, Chair of Sociology & Criminology, and Founding Director of Gender Studies at Stonehill College in Massachusetts. She has published over thirty books, earning commercial and critical success in both nonfiction and fiction, and her work has been translated into numerous languages. Her recent titles include *The Oxford Handbook of Methods for Public Scholarship*; *Handbook of Arts-Based Research*; *Research Design: Quantitative, Qualitative, Mixed Methods, Arts-Based, and Community-Based Participatory Research Approaches; Method Meets Art: Arts-Based Research Practice, Third Edition; Fiction as Research Practice; The Oxford Handbook of Qualitative Research, Second Edition*; and the novels *Shooting Stars, Twinkle, Spark, Film, Blue, American Circumstance*, and *Low-Fat Love*. She is also series creator and editor for ten book series with Oxford University Press, Brill | Sense, and Guilford Press, and is cofounder and co-editor-in-chief of *Art/Research International: A Transdisciplinary Journal*. A vocal advocate for public scholarship, she has blogged for numerous outlets, and is frequently called upon by the US national news media. In addition to receiving numerous honors for her books, including American Fiction Awards, USA Best Book Awards, and a Living Now Book Award, she has received career awards from the New England Sociological Association, the American Creativity Association, the American Educational Research Association, the International Congress of Qualitative Inquiry, and the National Art Education Association. In 2016, Mogul, a global women's empowerment network, named her an "Influencer." In 2018, the National Women's Hall of Fame honored her, and SUNY-New Paltz established the "Patricia Leavy Award for Art and Social Justice." Please visit www.patricialeavy.com for more information or for links to her social media.